The Hi Lo Cookbook

The Hi Lo Cookbook

High-Energy Low-Fat Recipes

Silvana Franco

Acknowledgements

My thanks to everyone involved in this great project: the talented Gareth and Lucy for making the book look so lovely and for being such fun to work with; my smashing assistant Fergal for his diligent testing and creative input; the wonderful Nicky and Rachel at BBC Books – thank you for asking me to do this book and for being so brilliant to work with; Sarah, Jerry and Julie at JHA who I love; my husband Robert, thanks for everything, everyday. And finally my son Fabio who was in my tummy, making me feel queasy, during the whole development of this book and thanks to whom I now have to follow my own advice, cook these recipes again and shift the extra two stone he gave me!

This book is published to accompany the UKTV television series entitled *The Hi Lo Club*, which was first broadcast in 2005.

Published by BBC Books, BBC Worldwide Ltd, Woodlands,
80 Wood Lane, London W12 0TT
First published 2005

ISBN 0 563 52155 4
Commissioning Editor: Nicky Ross
Project Editor: Rachel Copus
Copy Editor: Mari Roberts
Designer: Lisa Pettibone
Stylist: Lucy Pearce
Production Controller: Arlene Alexander

Set in Univers and Meta Plus
Printed and bound in Great Britain by The Bath Press
Colour origination by Butler and Tanner Ltd

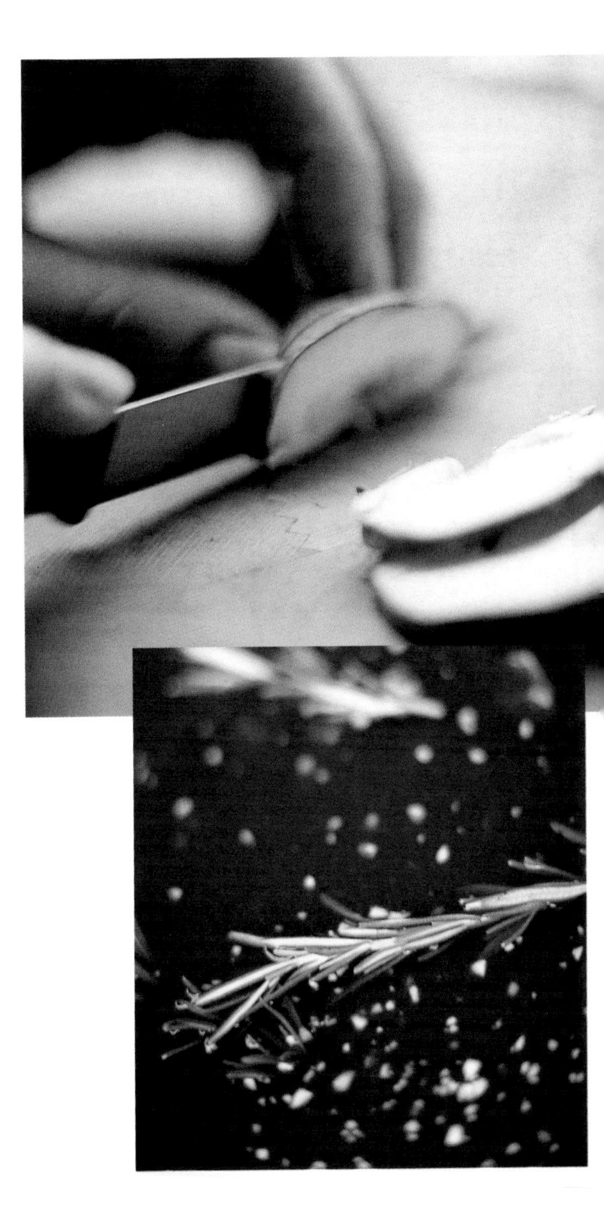

If you require further information on any BBC Worldwide product, please call 08700 777 001 or visit our website on www.bbcshop.com

If you would like further information on this or any other UKTV programme, please visit their website on www.ukfood.tv

All the spoon measurements in this book are level unless otherwise stated. A tablespoon is 15 ml; a teaspoon is 5 ml. Follow one set of measurements when preparing any of the recipes. Do not mix metric with imperial. All eggs used in the recipes are medium-sized. All vegetables should be peeled unless the recipe says otherwise.

Contents

Introduction

Whilst we all know the best way to manage our weight is with a good, balanced diet and plenty of exercise, it's not always quite so easy to put this theory into practice. The fact of the matter is that the body uses a certain amount of energy each day, dependant on various factors such as age, height, weight and activity levels, and if you eat more fuel (calories) than you use, your body will store it as fat. One of the first steps in the right direction is to reduce the amount of calorie-heavy fat you eat. By eating plenty of fruit and vegetables, and moderate amounts of protein and carbohydrates, you're three-quarters of the way towards a healthy, balanced diet. And cutting down on the fat should turn out to be a lot easier than you think.

The recipes in this book are all simple to follow and come with full nutritional information including calories and fat content. But most important of all, they are delicious and satisfying. The one thing guaranteed to make you want to give up any healthy-eating plan is when the food you eat is bland, repetitive and unsatisfying. These recipes are different – you could serve them at any mealtime, even a dinner party, and your guests will never know they are eating low-fat food. Each recipe is low in saturated fat (5 g or less per portion), low in salt (1.5 g or less) and/or low in added sugar (5 g or less).

Some recipes in the book are marked as **'super healthy'** – these have at least one of the following special health attributes as well:

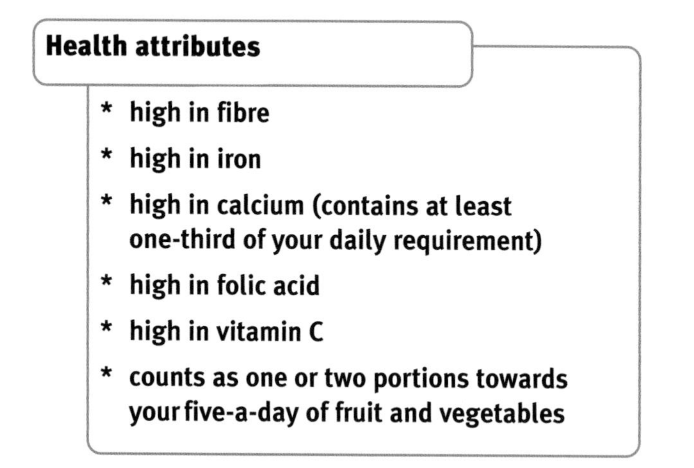

Health attributes
* high in fibre
* high in iron
* high in calcium (contains at least one-third of your daily requirement)
* high in folic acid
* high in vitamin C
* counts as one or two portions towards your five-a-day of fruit and vegetables

A healthy-eating plan

If you plan to embark on a full healthy-eating plan, then preparation and of course, determination, are the keys to success.

Plan your meals in advance – maybe make up a menu for the week ahead, including drinks and snacks. When shopping, write a strict list and stick to it. And remember what they always say – never go shopping when you're hungry as it becomes so hard to keep your resolve. If you have access to the Internet, all the major supermarkets now offer a very good service where you can get your groceries delivered to your home. Not only does this save you time (although pushing the trolley and carrying bags are all good exercise), it means you won't come into contact with the kind of foods you want to avoid, and that really does make a difference. If it's not in your cupboard in the first place, you can't eat it!

Try, if possible, to eat three filling meals a day, adding a healthy snack or two, if you feel you need to. Drink plenty of water and try taking advantage of the fantastic selection of herbal teas available. Limit your caffeine and alcohol consumption, though the odd glass of wine won't hurt much. But remember, alcohol does suppress your energy levels, and don't forget the 120 calories each glass contains.

Start as you mean to go on

If you start the day on the right foot – with a good, filling breakfast, you'll find yourself feeling energized and packed with vitality rather than distracted, peckish and inevitably reaching for the biscuit tin by 11a.m. Never, ever skip breakfast. The aim is to keep your body on an even keel

with a slow release of energy throughout the day rather than yo-yoing energy levels that leave you feeling lethargic and hungry. Stick to your balanced, low-fat diet, try to avoid stimulants such as caffeine (which also inhibits the absorption of vitamins and minerals), alcohol and chocolate as well, and you'll find it easier to focus on your long-term goal (and you'll skip a fair few calories along the way).

Snacking

Some of us do find it hard not to eat between meals and if that includes you, it's far better to have some healthy snacks on hand rather than trying to use willpower and ending up at the office vending machine because you just can't make it through until lunchtime.

Here are some suggestions of the kind of things you could keep in the fridge at home, or your desk drawer at work:

Fresh fruit – ready-to-eat or easy-to-peel – avoid oranges, as they just make too much mess

Dried fruit – small-sized snack packs of succulent ready-to-eat dried fruit are widely available

Cereal bars – check the nutritional info and go for ones under 120 calories

Wholemeal pitta and hummus – make your own hummus (page 21, step one) or look for the reduced-calorie versions in the supermarket

Rye crackerbreads and cottage cheese – eat these with a celery stalk and/or a couple of carrot sticks for a satisfying snack

Pick-and-mix cheeses – go for softer cheese, such as Brie wedges or light Mini Babybel, rather than full-fat hard types. Not the lowest-fat option but a good source of protein and calcium

Rice cakes – snack packs now come in lots of flavours

Pure fruit or yoghurt-based smoothies – make your own (see page 13) or buy one of the additive-free ones available

Low-fat fruity yoghurts or, my favourite, mini fromage frais – they might be aimed at children but they're scrumptious, low-fat, sweetener-free and come in at around 80 calories

Air-popped corn – make it yourself using a popcorn machine or in a microwave (and don't add any oil or sugar!)

Top Ten Tips

* Drink lots of water – take a 1.5-litre (2½-pint) bottle of water to work with you and try to finish it all by home time

* Eat five portions of fruit and vegetables every day

* Never skip breakfast

* Plan your meals for the week ahead. Write a shopping list and stick to it – use the Internet if possible and never shop when you're hungry

* Keep a good supply of healthy snacks to hand

* Remove all visible fat from food before you cook it – take the skin off chicken and trim the white fat off any meat. Don't eat sausages (it's not visible from the outside but it's certainly there!)

* Limit stimulants such as caffeine, alcohol and refined sugar

* Limit the number of times you eat out to once a week. Take your own packed lunch to work or choose soup in the canteen

* Take your time. Don't cut out any food groups altogether, such as carbohydrates, in a bid to lose weight quickly – your body needs balance. And don't do denial – you'll only end up cracking and a little bit of what you fancy does you good. I keep a jar of miniature chocolates on the top shelf of my storecupboard for when I really fancy a bit of a treat

* Only eat things you like the taste of – find what works for you and don't force yourself to eat things just because they're good for you

* And finally…enjoy these lovely recipes – cooking should never be stressful and eating should always be a pleasure

SERVES 12

- 200 g (7 oz) jumbo porridge oats
- 100 g (4 oz) rye or wheat flakes
- 75 g (3 oz) unblanched almonds, roughly chopped
- 100 g (4 oz) desiccated coconut
- 150 g (5 oz) mixed raisins and sultanas

Morning Munch Muesli

Home-made muesli is wonderful. I've kept this unsweetened as sugar attracts moisture, so it will last longer without it – just add sugar to taste when you eat it. Make a batch once a week or so and store in an airtight container. Serve with milk or yoghurt and some fresh fruit such as bananas and raspberries.

1 Preheat the oven to 160°C/325°F/Gas 3. Mix together the oats, rye or wheat flakes and almonds and spread out over a large baking sheet. Bake for 15 minutes, until toasted, then stir in the coconut and return to the oven for another 5 minutes, until golden. Leave to cool.

2 Stir in the dried fruit and store in an airtight container until ready to serve.

Nutrition notes per serving
Calories **213** Protein **5.7 g** Carbohydrate **27 g** Fat **10 g** Saturated fat **5 g** Fibre **4.6 g** Added sugars **none** Salt **0.02 g**

SERVES 4

2 bananas

1 small mango, peeled and cubed

10 ready-to-eat dried apricots, roughly chopped

600 ml (1 pint) freshly squeezed orange juice

SUPER HEALTHY

Four-fruit Smoothie

Smoothies and fresh juices are at their vitamin-packed best as soon as they're made, so whiz these up to order rather than making them in advance and chilling them.

1 Peel the bananas and break them into a liquidizer. Add the mango, apricots and a splash of the juice and whiz until smooth.

2 Add the remaining juice and whiz again until thick and frothy. Pour into ice-filled glasses and drink straight away.

Nutrition notes per serving
Calories **176** Protein **3.0 g** Carbohydrate **43 g** Fat **0.4 g** Saturated fat **0.1 g** Fibre **4.1 g** Added sugars **none** Salt **0.02 g**

SERVES 2

150 g (5 oz) frozen summer berries

150 g carton low-fat natural yoghurt

150 ml (5 fl oz) apple juice

Summer Berry Slush

Bags of frozen berries provide summer flavours all year round – and this drink has slushy-ice texture so it's truly refreshing.

1 Place the frozen fruit in a liquidizer with the yoghurt and apple juice and whiz until slushy. Pour into glasses and serve straight away.

Nutrition notes per serving
Calories **92** Protein **4.5 g** Carbohydrate **17 g** Fat **1 g** Saturated fat **0.5 g** Fibre **2 g** Added sugars **none** Salt **0.17 g**

SERVES 4

- 1 small, round ripe melon, such as Ogen, Charentais or Galia, skinned, seeded and cubed
- 150 g (5 oz) plump and firm red grapes
- grated rind and juice of 1 lime
- handful of ice cubes

SUPER HEALTHY

Melon and Red Grape Salad

Eating fresh fruit salad is one of the very best ways to make sure you start the day with a spring in your step. I find that firm fruit such as pear and apple can be a bit heavy-going first thing in the morning, and prefer to opt for a mix of soft and juicy (melon) and crisp and juicy (grapes), tied together with zing (lime).

1 Toss together the melon, grapes, lime rind and juice and ice cubes. Eat at once.

Nutrition notes per serving
Calories **42** Protein **0.6 g** Carbohydrate **10 g** Fat **0.1 g** Saturated fat **none** Fibre **0.3 g** Added sugars **none** Salt **0.06 g**

Nutrition notes per serving
Calories **155** Protein **12.2 g** Carbohydrate **6 g** Fat **9.4 g** Saturated fat **2.4 g** Fibre **0.2 g** Added sugars **5.3 g** Salt **0.99 g**

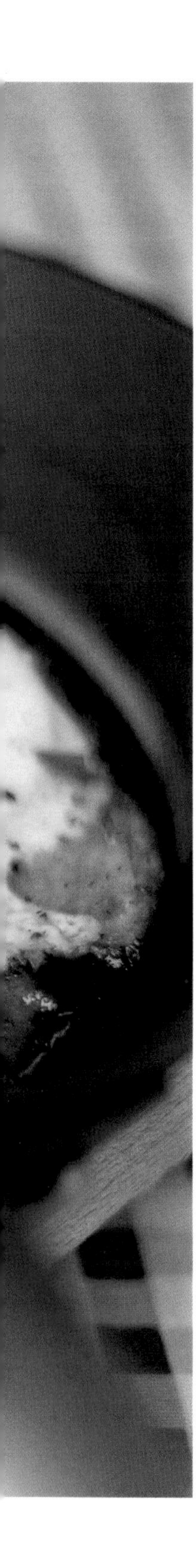

SERVES 1

tiny splash of olive oil

thick slice of ham, about 25 g (1 oz)

1 tsp caster sugar

1 tbsp red wine vinegar

1 large egg

1 tsp chopped fresh parsley or snipped chives

salt and freshly ground black pepper

crusty bread, to serve

Continental Ham and Eggs

Bring the Mediterranean to your breakfast table with this special dish for one. I have flameproof terracotta dishes that I bought on holiday which are perfect for cooking and eating out of, but a small, non-stick frying pan will do just as well.

1 Heat the oil in a flameproof dish or pan. Once hot, cook the ham for a few seconds on each side then remove.

2 Add the sugar to the pan and once it melts and begins to turn golden, add the vinegar. Bubble for a few seconds then return the ham. Crack in the egg and season with salt and pepper. Cook until the egg is done to your liking then scatter over the parsley or chives and eat at once with crusty bread.

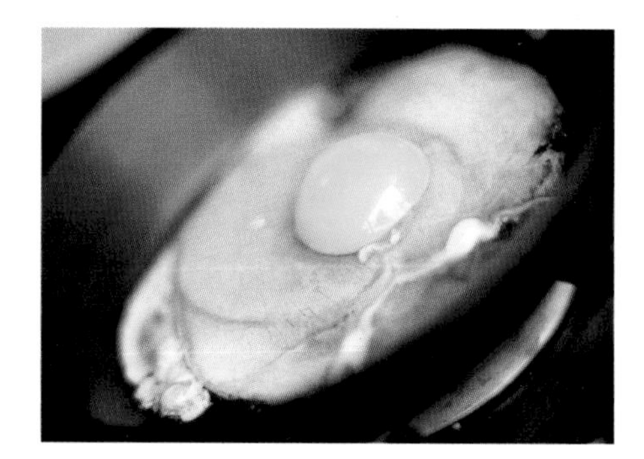

SERVES 2–4

2 orange or red peppers
400 g can chopped tomatoes
1 garlic clove, crushed
pinch or so of cayenne, plus extra for sprinkling
pinch of muscovado sugar
1 tsp olive oil
4 small eggs
salt and freshly ground black pepper
hot toast, to serve

SUPER HEALTHY

Saucy Eggs and Tomatoes

This makes a lovely relaxed breakfast for four, or a casual supper for two.

1 Cook the peppers under a hot grill for 15 minutes, turning from time to time until the skins blister and char.

2 Meanwhile, place the tomatoes, garlic, cayenne, sugar and olive oil in a frying pan with 150 ml (5 fl oz) water and some salt and pepper and bubble gently together.

3 Transfer the peppers to a plate, cover with a tea towel and set aside for 5 minutes. Then skin them, halve and seed them, and cut the flesh into strips about 1 cm (½ inch) wide. Add the pepper strips to the pan.

4 Make four wells in the mixture and crack an egg into each. Bubble gently until the eggs are just cooked. Sprinkle over a little more cayenne and serve swiftly with hot toast.

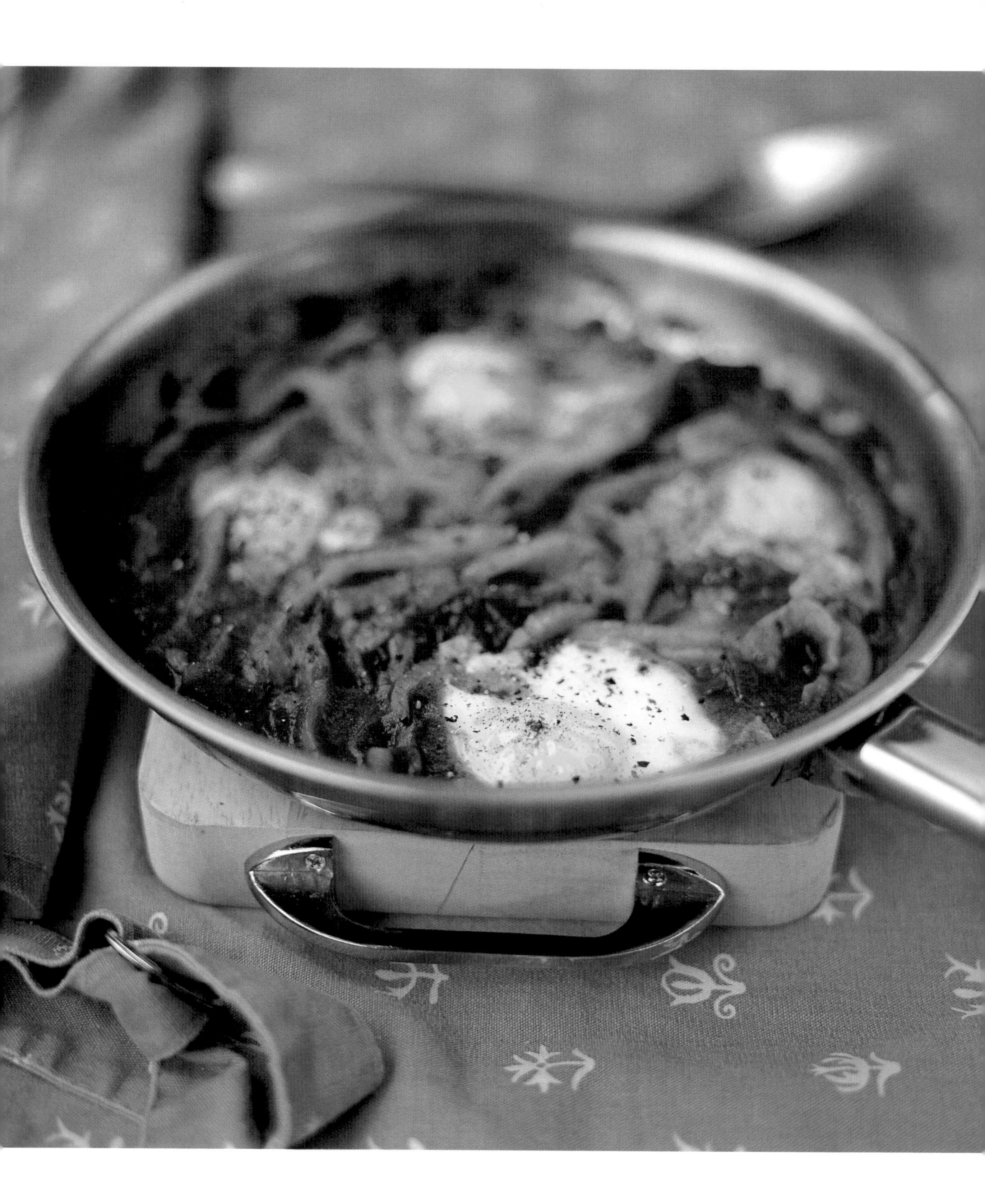

Nutrition notes per serving
Calories **124** Protein **8.4 g** Carbohydrate **8 g** Fat **6.6 g** Saturated fat **1.6 g** Fibre **2.3 g** Added sugars **0.5 g** Salt **0.39 g**

Avocado Hummus

A vitamin-packed, flavour-bursting cross between hummus and guacamole. Fantastic on toast for breakfast or as a dip for crudités or strips of warm flatbread.

1 Place the chickpeas in a food processor with the garlic and whiz until very finely chopped. Add 75 ml/3 fl oz cold water and whiz again until smooth and soft.

2 Meanwhile, halve and stone the avocado then scrape out the flesh and mash with a fork. Add to the food processor and pulse until well blended. The mixture should be soft not stiff, so add more water if it needs it.

3 Stir in the lime juice, mint and salt and pepper to taste. Cover and chill until needed.

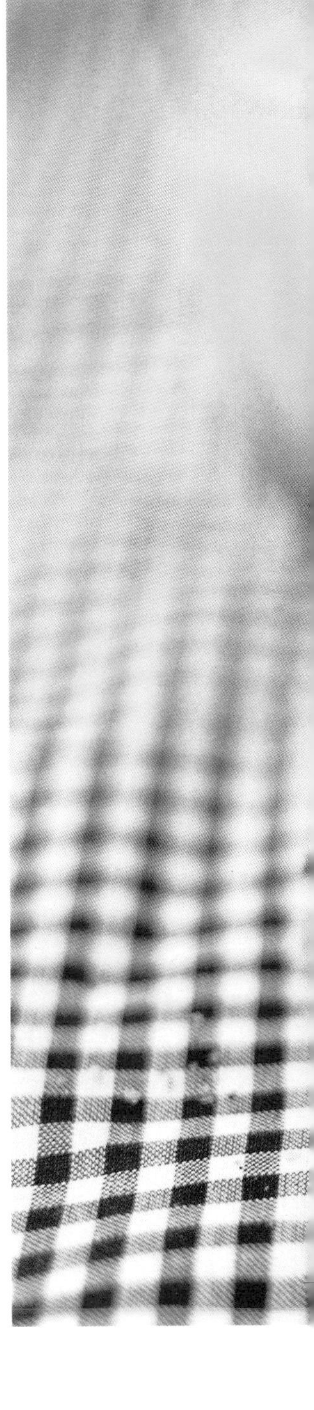

Nutrition notes per serving
Calories **104** Protein **3.6 g** Carbohydrate **7 g** Fat **6.9 g** Saturated fat **0.7 g** Fibre **2.7 g**
Added sugars **none** Salt **0.23 g**

SERVES 6

- 400 g can chickpeas, drained
- 1 small garlic clove, peeled and roughly chopped
- 1 large ripe avocado
- juice of 1 plump lime
- handful of fresh mint, finely chopped
- salt and freshly ground black pepper

Nutrition notes per bun
Calories **124** Protein **3.8 g** Carbohydrate **27 g** Fat **0.8 g** Saturated fat **0.3 g** Fibre **0.8 g** Added sugars **4.1 g** Salt **0.28 g**

MAKES 9 BUNS

- pinch of saffron threads
- 200 ml (8 fl oz) warm milk
- 500 g (1 lb 2 oz) strong white flour
- 7 g sachet easy-blend yeast
- 1 tsp table salt
- 1 tsp mixed spice
- 1 egg, beaten
- 50 g (2 oz) dried cranberries and/or blueberries
- 50 g (2 oz) small sultanas
- grated rind of 1 lemon
- 50 g (2 oz) golden caster sugar, plus 2 tbsp for the glaze

Dulwich Buns

My version of the Chelsea bun. This makes a wonderful breakfast-time pastry which, unlike a classic Danish, is not packed with butter. Serve still warm from the oven with a skinny latte for a very cosmopolitan start to the day.

1 Stir the saffron into the milk and set aside for a few minutes.

2 In a large bowl, mix together the flour, yeast, salt and spice. Make a well in the centre and pour in the warm saffron milk and beaten egg then stir together to make a soft dough. If the dough feels hard or dry, you will need to add a little more milk. Knead on a floured surface for 5 minutes or so until smooth, then return to the bowl, cover and leave in a warm place for one hour until well risen. Alternatively, cover the bowl and chill overnight.

3 Briefly knead the dough then roll it out to a rectangle 40 x 20 cm (16 x 8 inches). Leaving a border of 0.5 cm (¼ inch) round the edges, sprinkle over the fruit, lemon rind and sugar. Roll up from the short side, like a Swiss roll. Slice the roll into nine even pieces then arrange them together in a 20-cm (8-inch) square cake tin (or a rectangular tin of 20 x 30 cm/ 8 x 12 inches), allowing the edges of the buns to touch. Cover again and leave to rise for 30 minutes until well risen. This may take a little longer if the dough was chilled overnight.

4 Preheat the oven to 200°C/400°F/Gas 6. Mix together the remaining sugar with two tablespoons of water. Bake the buns for 20–25 minutes until golden and cooked through. Brush them with the sugar water as soon as they come out of the oven. Serve warm or leave to cool before serving.

SERVES 6

200 g (7 oz) strong wholemeal flour

200 g (7 oz) plain flour, plus extra for kneading and dusting

1 tsp salt

2 tbsp caster sugar

1 tsp bicarbonate of soda

2 ripe bananas

250 ml (9 fl oz) buttermilk or 250 g (9 oz) low-fat natural yoghurt

100 ml (4 fl oz) semi-skimmed milk

Banana Soda Farls

I love soda bread – it has a fantastic flavour and is much quicker and easier to make than most breads. I've added mashed banana to this recipe, and I like to serve it warm for breakfast. Alternatively, allow the wedges to cool, split in half, toast and drizzle with honey.

1 Preheat the oven to 220°C/425°F/Gas 7. Mix the flours, salt, sugar and bicarbonate of soda in a large bowl.

2 Peel the bananas and mash them to a pulp. Add to the flour with the buttermilk or yoghurt and enough semi-skimmed milk to make a firm (but not dry) dough. Knead lightly until smooth, then shape into a 23-cm (9-inch) round.

3 Cut the round into six wedges. Transfer to a non-stick baking sheet and sprinkle with a little flour. Bake for 20–30 minutes until browned and crusty. Cool on a wire rack.

Nutrition notes per serving
Calories **300** Protein **10 g** Carbohydrate **65 g** Fat **1.8 g** Saturated fat **0.5 g** Fibre **4.5 g** Added sugars **5.3 g** Salt **1.5 g**

SERVES 8

- 300 g (11 oz) mashing (floury) potatoes, such as Maris Piper or King Edward, peeled and cubed
- 7 g sachet easy-blend yeast
- 1 tsp table salt
- 1 tbsp chopped fresh rosemary
- 1 tbsp olive oil
- 700 g (1 lb 9 oz) strong plain flour, plus extra for kneading
- 200 g (7 oz) polenta or fine cornmeal
- 300–450 ml (1/2–3/4 pint) warm water
- 2 tbsp milk

Rosemary Polenta Bread

This is a hearty bread made with potatoes and cornmeal: a brilliant source of slow-release energy. Best eaten on the day it's made, but it can also be served toasted over the next few days.

1 Cook the potatoes in a large pan of boiling salted water for 15 minutes or so until tender. Drain them well then mash them thoroughly. Stir in the yeast, salt, rosemary, oil, flour, polenta and enough water to make a soft dough. Knead vigorously for 5 minutes, adding flour when necessary, to make a smooth dough. Cover with a clean tea towel and leave for 1½ hours in a warm place until doubled in size.

2 Knead briefly then shape into a neat oval loaf, pinching the edges to give slightly pointed ends. Using a sharp knife, make a deep slash lengthways down the loaf, then leave in a warm place for 30 minutes or so until well risen. Preheat the oven to 200°C/400°F/Gas 6.

3 Brush the loaf with the milk then bake for 45 minutes until golden brown and cooked through. Cool on a wire rack.

Nutrition notes per serving
Calories **434** Protein **13.9 g** Carbohydrate **92 g** Fat **3.6 g** Saturated fat **0.6 g** Fibre **3.8 g** Added sugars **none** Salt **1.27 g**

SOUPS **SOUPS** SOUPS **SOUPS** SOUPS **SOUPS** SOUPS **SOUPS** SOUPS **SOU**

SERVES 4

- 1 tsp olive oil
- 2 lean back bacon rashers, chopped
- 2 garlic cloves, finely chopped
- 2 celery sticks, finely chopped
- 1 large carrot, finely chopped
- 2 floury potatoes, such as Maris Piper, peeled and diced
- 400 g can borlotti or cannellini beans, drained
- 1.5 litres (2½ pints) hot chicken or vegetable stock
- 250 g (9 oz) leaf spinach
- salt and freshly ground black pepper

Rustic Italian Bean and Spinach Soup

A spin on the wonderful, classic Italian *ribollita*, which takes hours to make. This is on the table in roughly 30 minutes (give or take a few minutes for prep), thanks to canned beans and the quick-cook nature of spinach. Delicious!

1 Place the oil, bacon, garlic, celery and carrot in a large pan and cook gently for 5 minutes. Add the potatoes, beans and hot stock, bring to the boil and simmer for 20–25 minutes until the potatoes are very tender.

2 Add the spinach and cook for a couple of minutes until wilted. Add salt and pepper to taste then ladle into bowls and serve.

Nutrition notes per serving
Calories **175** Protein **12 g** Carbohydrate **27 g** Fat **3 g** Saturated fat **0.5 g** Fibre **6.5 g**
Added sugars **none** Salt **2.6 g**

Nutrition notes per serving
Calories **216** Protein **23.4 g** Carbohydrate **23 g** Fat **3.9 g** Saturated fat **1.4 g** Fibre **2.2 g** Added sugars **none** Salt **0.32 g**

SERVES 4

4 whole chicken thighs
2 tomatoes, roughly chopped
1 carrot, peeled and cubed
2 celery stalks, roughly chopped
1 shallot, roughly chopped
2 garlic cloves, roughly chopped
2 bay leaves, fresh or dried
1/2 tsp fennel seeds
100 g (4 oz) very small pasta shapes: stars (*stellini*) and melon seeds (*seme di melone*) are my favourites
handful of fresh parsley, roughly chopped
1 tbsp freshly grated Parmesan
sea salt and freshly ground black pepper

Chicken and Pastina Broth

A nutritious, tasty and economical soup – this is one of the dishes I learned to cook in my mum's kitchen, and it helped me and my flatmates and boyfriends survive our student years. Now that I've got my own family to feed, I still like to make it. I also often use a chicken carcass, once I've cut all the meat off for another dish.

1 Skin the chicken thighs and cut off the strip of fat that runs down the side. Place the thighs in a large pan with the tomatoes, carrot, celery, shallot, garlic, bay leaves and fennel seeds.

2 Cover with 1.75 litres (3 pints) of water. Bring to the boil and simmer gently for 1 hour.

3 Lift out the chicken thighs, and pass the soup mixture through a strong wire sieve into a clean pan, pushing as much cooked vegetable through as possible.

4 Using two forks, shred the chicken meat off the bones and add to the broth. Check the seasoning, adding salt and pepper, and bring to a gentle simmer. At this point you can cool the broth for reheating and serving later.

5 Cook the pasta in a pan of boiling salted water for 5 minutes or so, following the packet instructions. Drain then divide between four bowls. Ladle over the hot broth, top each serving with chopped parsley, a pinch of Parmesan and plenty of black pepper, and serve.

Curried Lentil and Lime Soup

Curry paste is made using vegetable oil but it has loads more flavour and none of the harshness of curry powder, so I think it's worth sacrificing a few calories for. If you choose to substitute powder for paste, please do fry it in a little oil for a few minutes to take away the rawness of the spices.

1 Place the curry paste, onion, garlic, ginger and cumin seeds in a large pan and cook gently together for 3 minutes.

2 Add the lentils and stock, bring to the boil and simmer gently for 20 minutes. Add the sultanas and cook for a further 10 minutes. Add the lime rind and juice, and salt and pepper to taste.

3 Ladle into bowls and top each serving with a large spoonful of yoghurt and a sprinkling of mint. Serve with warm chapattis.

Nutrition notes per serving
Calories **241** Protein **15.4 g** Carbohydrate **43 g** Fat **1.9 g** Saturated fat **0.1 g** Fibre **3.2 g** Added sugars **none** Salt **0.28 g**

SERVES 4

1 tbsp hot curry paste

1 onion, finely chopped

2 garlic cloves, finely chopped

4-cm (1½-inch) piece of root ginger, peeled and finely chopped

1 tsp cumin seeds

200 g (7 oz) red lentils

1.5 litres (2½ pints) chicken or vegetable stock

50 g (2 oz) small sultanas

grated rind and juice of 1 lime

150 g carton fat-free natural yoghurt

2 tbsp chopped fresh mint

sea salt and freshly ground black pepper

4 warm chapattis, to serve

SERVES 4

- 750 g (1 lb 11 oz) butternut squash or small pumpkin, peeled, seeded and cubed
- 500 g (1 lb 2 oz) ripe tomatoes, quartered
- 2 garlic cloves, quartered
- 1 tsp olive oil
- 2 chillies, halved, seeded and roughly chopped
- 2 tsp ground ginger
- 1 tsp dark muscovado sugar
- 1.75 litres (3 pints) hot chicken or vegetable stock
- salt and freshly ground black pepper

Roasted Pumpkin and Tomato Chowder

Pumpkin roasts and purées into a most satisfying, thick-textured soup. It is also rich in vitamin A, which is essential for growth, healthy skin and hair, good vision and healthy tooth enamel.

1 Preheat the oven to 200°C/400°F/Gas 6. Place the pumpkin, tomatoes and garlic in a large deep roasting tin. Season well with salt and pepper, drizzle over the oil and roast for 30 minutes until the pumpkin feels tender when pierced with a knife.

2 Sprinkle over the chillies, ginger and sugar, then pour over the hot stock. Return to the oven for 20 minutes. Purée roughly with a potato masher or blitz with a hand-held blender, depending on how smooth you would like your chowder. Serve warm.

Nutrition notes per serving
Calories **124** Protein **5.4 g** Carbohydrate **24 g** Fat **1.6 g** Saturated fat **0.2 g** Fibre **4.4 g** Added sugars **1.3 g** Salt **1.49 g**

SERVES 4

- 3 lemongrass stalks
- 1.5 litres (2½ pints) chicken stock
- 5 kaffir lime leaves, shredded
- 2 shallots, thinly sliced
- 5-cm (2-inch) piece of root ginger, peeled and thinly sliced
- 2 tbsp fish sauce
- 2 tbsp chilli sauce
- 200 g (7 oz) shiitake mushrooms, thinly sliced
- 16 raw tiger prawns, shelled and de-veined, tail section intact
- 4 red bird's-eye chillies, thinly sliced, seeds and all
- juice of 2 limes
- 4 spring onions, thinly sliced
- handful of fresh coriander leaves

Tom Yam Goong (Thai Sour Prawn Soup)

An absolute classic! Warn your guests to spit out the pieces of lemongrass, lime leaf and prawn tails. Whether they choose to chew or spit the slices of ginger is up to them. If you want to make this broth more substantial, serve it with thin rice noodles – allow 25 g (1 oz) per person and reconstitute with boiling water according to packet instructions.

1 Bruise the lemongrass stalks with a rolling pin and place in a large pan with the stock, lime leaves, shallots, ginger, fish sauce and chilli sauce. Bring to the boil and simmer for 10 minutes.

2 Stir in the mushrooms, prawns and chillies and cook for a few minutes until the prawns are pink and curled.

3 Add lime juice to taste and ladle into bowls. Scatter over the spring onions and coriander leaves and serve steaming hot.

Nutrition notes per serving
Calories **72** Protein **12 g** Carbohydrate **5 g** Fat **0.8 g** Saturated fat **none** Fibre **0.3 g** Added sugars **0.5 g** Salt **3.42 g**

Super-speedy Pea Soup with Crispy Parma Ham

This is what I call an emergency dish for two. No time, no food in the cupboard? Well, if you're like me and always keep a bag of frozen peas in stock, this is the dish for you. The crème fraîche adds a touch of luxury but you can also make the soup without it.

1 Heat the olive oil in a large pan and cook the onion, chilli and garlic for 5 minutes until softened, adding the cumin seeds for the last minute.

2 Add the peas and hot stock and bring to the boil. Simmer for 2–3 minutes until the peas are tender.

3 Meanwhile, heat a sturdy non-stick frying pan. When hot, cook the ham over a high heat for 30 seconds on each side.

4 Take the soup off the heat and purée it using a hand-held blender. Stir in the crème fraiche and check the seasoning, adding a squeeze of fresh lemon juice and salt and pepper. Ladle the soup into bowls and break over the crispy ham. Serve with crusty bread or toast.

Nutrition notes per serving
Calories **272** Protein **20.9 g** Carbohydrate **29 g** Fat **8.9 g** Saturated fat **2.7 g** Fibre **13.4 g** Added sugars **none** Salt **1.75 g**

SERVES 2

- 2 tsp olive oil
- 1 small onion, roughly chopped
- 1 red chilli, seeded and roughly chopped
- 1 garlic clove, roughly chopped
- 1 tsp cumin seeds
- 500 g bag frozen peas
- 600 ml (1 pint) hot chicken stock
- 2 slices Parma ham
- 1–2 tbsp half-fat crème fraîche
- 1/2 lemon
- salt and freshly ground black pepper
- crusty bread or toast, to serve

Nutrition notes per serving
Calories **82** Protein **5.9 g** Carbohydrate **9 g** Fat **2 g** Saturated fat **0.3 g** Fibre **2.9 g** Added sugars **none** Salt **1.02 g**

SERVES 4

1 tsp olive oil

1 onion, finely chopped

2 garlic cloves, finely chopped

2 fresh thyme sprigs

750g (1 lb 11 oz) brown mushrooms, sliced

1 white potato, peeled and diced

1.2 litres (2 pints) hot chicken or vegetable stock

2 tbsp Marsala, Madeira or medium sherry

salt and freshly ground black pepper

FOR THE CHESHIRE CHEESE CROÛTES (optional)

8 x 1-cm (1/2-inch) slices of baguette

75 g (3 oz) Cheshire cheese, grated

few shakes of Worcestershire sauce

Really Simple Brown Mushroom Soup

Brown mushrooms, such as Portobello or chestnut, seem to have more flavour than the traditional white variety, and they also cook down to make a lovely rich-tasting soup. I like to serve this soup with some croûtes, ideally cheese-topped as cheese is so good partnered with mushrooms, though, of course, that is going to push up the fat content of your meal. The calorie count here is for the soup alone, which means if you want to include the Cheshire cheese croûtes (and I think you should) you'll need to add on 127 kcal and 6.4 g of fat per serving. And remember, most brands of Worcestershire sauce are not suitable for vegetarians.

1 Heat the oil in a large pan and very gently cook the onion, garlic and thyme for about 10 minutes until nicely softened. Add the mushrooms and potato and cook for a further 5 minutes.

2 Pour in the stock, bring to the boil and simmer gently for 20 minutes. Lift out the thyme stalks, then purée the soup using a hand-held blender or liquidize it until smooth. Add the Marsala and season to taste. Ladle into bowls and serve.

3 For the croûtes, simply toast the bread on one side under the grill, turn, sprinkle the cheese over the untoasted side, splash over a couple of drops of Worcestershire sauce, and melt the cheese under the grill. Serve bubbling with the hot soup.

Moroccan Carrot and Orange Soup

Carrot with cumin is a match made in heaven. I love carrots steamed, sliced and dressed with roasted cumin seeds, lemon juice and coriander leaves, and these same flavours also work together wonderfully in a soup. I've added orange juice because it has an evocative Moroccan flavour and aroma, and it brings out the natural sweetness of the carrots.

1 Place the ground cumin in a large saucepan and heat gently for 1–2 minutes until it just begins to darken and give off its aroma. Add the stock, carrots, potato, onion and garlic. Bring to the boil and simmer gently for 20 minutes.

2 Stir in the orange juice, season to taste and heat through thoroughly. You may choose to serve the soup as it is or liquidize it for a smooth texture.

3 Ladle the soup into bowls and sprinkle the surface with coriander leaves and cumin seeds.

Nutrition notes per serving
Calories **126** Protein **4.7 g** Carbohydrate **26 g** Fat **1.1 g** Saturated fat **0.1 g** Fibre **4 g** Added sugars **none** Salt **1.33 g**

SERVES 6

- 1 tsp ground cumin
- 1.5 litres (2½ pints) hot vegetable stock
- 4 large carrots, grated
- 1 large white potato, grated
- 1 onion, finely chopped
- 2 garlic cloves, crushed
- juice of 4 oranges, about 350 ml (generous ½ pint)
- salt and freshly ground black pepper
- large handful of fresh coriander leaves
- 1 tsp cumin seeds

SERVES 4

2 litres ($3\frac{1}{2}$ pints) vegetable stock
100 g (4 oz) long-grain rice
1 small onion, finely chopped
2 garlic cloves, finely chopped
4 fresh rosemary sprigs
3 courgettes, grated
juice and grated rind of 1 lemon
salt and freshly ground black pepper

Courgette, Lemon and Rice Soup

Rice is a great thickener for soups – in order for it to work, it needs to be cooked for longer than usual so that it breaks down and releases its starch. This soup is made with courgettes and lemon and I think it tastes rather Greek. You could take that theme a step further and add a spoonful of thick Greek yoghurt to each bowlful, if you fancy it.

1 Place the stock, rice, onion, garlic and rosemary in a large pan and bring to the boil. Simmer, uncovered, for 40 minutes.

2 Add the courgettes and cook for a further 5 minutes, then stir in the lemon rind and add salt, pepper and lemon juice to taste. Stir well, ladle into bowls and serve. Yum.

Nutrition notes per serving
Calories **132** Protein **6.1 g** Carbohydrate **26 g** Fat **0.9 g** Saturated fat **0.1 g** Fibre **1.2 g** Added sugars **none** Salt **1.65 g**

SERVES 4

- 4 vacuum-packed beetroot, about 250 g (9 oz) in total, cubed
- 8-cm (3-inch) piece of cucumber, peeled and cubed
- 1 red chilli, seeded and chopped
- 2 tbsp red wine or sherry vinegar
- 4 slices of white bread, crusts removed
- 1 red onion, finely chopped
- 4 ripe tomatoes, finely chopped
- 2 garlic cloves, finely chopped
- 4 tbsp chopped fresh parsley
- 2 tsp olive oil
- salt and freshly ground black pepper

Chilled Summer Beetroot Soup

I've never been crazy about chilled soups but this one is different. It's lovely hot but absolutely delicious chilled.

1 Place the beetroot, cucumber, chilli and 1.5 litres (2½ pints) of cold water in a liquidizer and blend until smooth – you will probably have to do this in two batches. Pass through a fine strainer into a large jug then stir in the vinegar and season generously. Chill until ready to serve.

2 Tear one slice of bread into each bowl then scatter over the red onion, tomatoes and garlic. Pour over the chilled soup, sprinkle over the parsley and drizzle each serving with a splash of oil.

Nutrition notes per serving
Calories **156** Protein **5.9 g** Carbohydrate **29 g** Fat **2.7 g** Saturated fat **0.4 g** Fibre **3.4 g** Added sugars **none** Salt **0.67 g**

SERVES 4

- 3 tbsp soy sauce
- 3 tbsp rice wine (sake) or dry sherry
- 2 tbsp dark muscovado sugar
- 4 x 100 g (4 oz) salmon fillets
- 250 g (9 oz) rice noodles (or Thai fragrant rice)
- 400 g (14 oz) asparagus spears or green beans, steamed, to serve

Teriyaki Salmon

Salmon is a robust fish that is a good match for Oriental flavours. This dish, like many Japanese dishes, tastes very clean and healthy without lacking flavour. Look out for packets of miso soup in Oriental stores or large supermarkets: it can be made up with boiling water, tastes delicious, is low in fat and makes a lovely accompaniment to this dish. This recipe also works well with chicken.

1 Place the soy sauce, rice wine, sugar and one tablespoon of water in a small saucepan and heat together gently, stirring until the sugar dissolves. Remove from the heat and allow to cool.

2 Place the salmon in a small shallow dish. Pour over the sauce and leave to marinate for at least 10 minutes or as long as 2 hours.

3 Cook the noodles (or rice) in a pan of boiling water according to packet instructions.

4 Preheat a griddle pan or heavy non-stick frying pan and cook the salmon for 3–4 minutes on each side until just cooked through and nicely browned.

5 Spoon the noodles or rice onto plates and serve with the teriyaki salmon and steamed greens.

Nutrition notes per serving
Calories **434** Protein **25.4 g** Carbohydrate **58 g** Fat **11.5 g** Saturated fat **2.3 g** Fibre **1.0 g** Added sugars **8.1 g** Salt **2.16 g**

SERVES 4

1 onion, roughly chopped
2 garlic cloves, halved
bunch of parsley
pinch of saffron threads
200 ml (7 fl oz) dry white wine
750 ml (1¼ pints) boiling water
1 chicken stock cube
1 kg (2 lb) live mussels, scrubbed and bearded
splash of olive oil
4 ripe tomatoes, chopped
400 g (14 oz) white fish, such as coley or haddock, cut into good-sized cubes
300 g (11 oz) cooked prawns, head and shell still on
sea salt and freshly ground black pepper

FOR THE GARLIC TOASTS
4 slices of country bread
2 unpeeled garlic cloves, halved

Mediterranean Fish Stew with Garlic Toasts

This luxurious dish makes a stunning dinner-party main course and none of your guests could possibly guess that it's a low-fat creation. I've left the shells on the prawns and mussels, so be prepared to use your fingers when it comes to the eating.

1 Place the onion, garlic, stalks from the parsley, saffron and white wine in a large pan. Bring to boil and bubble rapidly until reduced by half. Add the water and stock cube and bring to the boil. Add the mussels to the pan, cover with a lid and cook for 5 minutes. Check to see that all the shells have opened (there will be a couple that haven't), then strain the mussels into a colander set over another pan.

2 In the hot and now empty first pan, add the olive oil and tomatoes and cook for 2–3 minutes until the tomatoes are softened and pulpy – this stage is crucial, because if you simply add the tomatoes to the liquid without softening them first, they won't break down and you will have lumpy bits of tomato floating around in the stew, which is not so nice. You only need to use the smallest splash of oil when pulping them, just enough to stop them sticking.

3 Once the tomatoes have softened, return the strained stock to the pan, removing any stray parsley stalks that may have got through the colander, and bring to a gentle simmer.

4 Meanwhile, check through the mussels, discarding the few that haven't opened.

5 Add the fish and prawns to the pan and cook for 2 minutes, then add the cooked mussels for a further 2 minutes. Meanwhile, chop the parsley leaves. Check that the stew is

piping hot and the fish is cooked through. Add pepper and salt, if you need any, and the parsley, then ladle into large bowls, trying to ensure each serving gets a good selection of seafood.

6 Toast or griddle the bread and serve straight away, giving each guest a cut clove of garlic to rub over the surface.

Nutrition notes per serving
Calories **287** Protein **46 g** Carbohydrate **8 g** Fat **4.4 g** Saturated fat **0.6 g** Fibre **1.6 g** Added sugars **none** Salt **4.90 g**

Fluffy Smoked Haddock Potato Pie

Comfort food at its best – serve midweek with baked beans in front of the TV, or smarten up with a *pomodorino* (baby plum tomato) and rocket salad for the weekend.

1 Cook the potatoes in a large pan of boiling water for 15 minutes or so until tender.

2 Meanwhile, place the haddock in a pan, pour over the milk and sprinkle over the spring onions. Cover, bring to the boil and simmer for 5–8 minutes until the fish is cooked – it should flake easily. Lift out the cooked fish and discard the skin and any bones. Pour the warm milk and spring onions into a jug – you'll need 200 ml (7 fl oz) and there should easily be enough.

3 Drain the potatoes well and mash – ideally with a ricer – until smooth. Beat in the warm milk and spring onions, followed by the fromage frais. Gently fold in the flaked fish and check the seasoning – you're unlikely to need much, if any, salt, but grind in plenty of black pepper.

4 Spoon the mixture into a large, shallow heatproof dish and scatter over the cheese. Pop under a medium–low grill for 15 minutes until golden and crunchy on the surface.

Nutrition notes per serving
Calories **334** Protein **30.7 g** Carbohydrate **48 g** Fat **3.3 g** Saturated fat **1.5 g** Fibre **3.5 g** Added sugars **none** Salt **2.15 g**

SERVES 6

- 1.5 kg (3 lb) floury potatoes, such as Maris Piper or King Edwards, peeled and diced
- 600 g (1 lb 6 oz) undyed smoked haddock fillets
- 300 ml (1/2 pint) skimmed milk
- bunch of spring onions, finely chopped
- 200 g carton fat-free fromage frais
- 40 g (1 1/2 oz) finely grated Emmenthal or Leerdammer
- sea salt and freshly ground black pepper

Nutrition notes per serving
Calories **131** Protein **21.0 g** Carbohydrate **8 g** Fat **1.9 g** Saturated fat **0.3 g** Fibre **2 g** Added sugars **0.7 g** Salt **1.21 g**

SERVES 4

1 garlic clove, roughly chopped

3-cm (1-inch) piece of fresh root ginger, grated

1 fresh mild red chilli, seeded and roughly chopped

250 g (9 oz) fillet white fish, such as hoki, coley or cod, cubed

200 g (7 oz) shelled raw tiger prawns

2 tbsp chopped fresh coriander

sea salt and freshly ground black pepper

FOR THE SALAD

grated rind and juice of 1 lime

1 tbsp light soy sauce

1/2 tsp fish sauce

1/2 tsp caster sugar

1/2 Chinese leaf cabbage

2 carrots

1 red onion, thinly sliced

50 g (2 oz) beansprouts

Prawn and Ginger Cakes with Crunchy Salad

These tender little fishcakes are flavoured with chilli and coriander and when served with a crunchy Asian coleslaw make a really well balanced and rather smart lunch or supper.

1 Preheat the oven to 200°C/400°F/Gas 6. Place the garlic, ginger and chilli in a food processor and whiz until finely minced. Add the fish and prawns and a little salt and pepper. Finally add the coriander and whiz again (if you add it at the beginning with the ginger it will turn the mixture green).

2 Wet your hands with cold water, give them a good shake, then shape the prawn mixture into 12 cakes. Transfer to a lined baking sheet and cook for 15 minutes until golden and cooked through.

3 Meanwhile, stir together the lime rind and juice, soy sauce, fish sauce and caster sugar and set aside.

4 Using a mandolin or big knife, finely slice the cabbage, then cut the carrots into long shreds. Toss together the cabbage, carrots, red onion, beansprouts and lime dressing. Pile onto plates and serve with the prawn and ginger cakes.

SERVES 2

4 eggs, separated
50 g (2 oz) fresh white breadcrumbs
75 g (3 oz) smoked salmon, torn into thin strips
2 tbsp snipped fresh chives
100 g (4 oz) tiny asparagus, trimmed
1 tsp olive oil
salt and freshly ground black pepper
salad, to serve

Smart Salmon and Asparagus Omelette

This is a lovely, simple supper dish for two.

1 In a large bowl, stir together the egg yolks, breadcrumbs, salmon, chives, asparagus and some salt and pepper.

2 Whisk the egg whites in a separate bowl until they form soft peaks, then gently fold into the egg yolk mixture.

3 Heat the oil in a non-stick 20-cm (8-inch) frying pan. Once hot, gently tip in the mixture and cook for 5 minutes until golden underneath. Pop the pan under a preheated grill for a couple of minutes until the omelette is golden and set on top. Serve hot, with salad.

Nutrition notes per serving
Calories **347** Protein **29.1 g** Carbohydrate **21 g** Fat **17 g** Saturated fat **4.2 g** Fibre **1.5 g** Added sugars **none** Salt **2.70 g**

SERVES 6

- 4 whole plaice fillets
- 1 ripe mango, peeled and cut into small dice
- 4 green chillies, seeded and finely chopped
- 1 red onion, finely chopped
- grated rind and juice of 1 lime
- handful of fresh mint leaves
- salt and freshly ground black pepper
- leafy salad, to serve

Plain Grilled Plaice with Zingy Mango Salsa

Flat fish like plaice take such a short time to cook that a high-heat method such as grilling always works well. Complement the simply cooked fish with a lively fruit salsa, such as this one.

1 Make the salsa first: stir together the mango, chillies, red onion and lime rind and juice. Season with salt and pepper and chill until ready to serve.

2 Season the plaice and cook skin-side first under a hot grill for just a minute or two on each side until cooked through. Divide between four plates.

3 Tear the mint into the salsa then spoon over and around the fish. Serve with a leafy green salad.

Nutrition notes per serving
Calories **155** Protein **22 g** Carbohydrate **13 g** Fat **2 g** Saturated fat **0.3 g** Fibre **2.4 g** Added sugars **none** Salt **0.39 g**

SERVES 4

- 350 g (12 oz) linguine or spaghetti
- 4 ripe tomatoes, roughly chopped
- 2 garlic cloves, finely chopped
- 1 red chilli, seeded and finely chopped
- 1 tsp olive oil
- 1 tsp sugar
- 170 g can white crabmeat, drained (120 g/4½ oz drained weight)
- grated rind and juice of 1 lemon
- handful of fresh basil leaves
- salt and freshly ground black pepper

Crab Linguine

Canned crab is just made for tossing with freshly cooked linguine or spaghetti. Keep a can in the store cupboard and you can knock this up in minutes. It also works brilliantly made with tuna canned in spring water.

1 Put a large pan of water on to boil for the pasta.

2 Place the tomatoes, garlic, chilli, olive oil and sugar in a small pan. Bubble together for 8–10 minutes until thickened and pulpy. Add the crabmeat and lemon rind, and heat gently until piping hot.

3 Meanwhile, salt the boiling water for the pasta and cook it according to packet instructions.

4 Season the crab mixture with salt, pepper and lemon juice, then tear in the basil leaves. Drain the pasta, toss with the crab mixture and divide between bowls.

Nutrition notes per serving
Calories **353** Protein **16.9 g** Carbohydrate **70 g** Fat **2.8 g** Saturated fat **0.4 g** Fibre **3.5 g** Added sugars **1.3 g** Salt **0.45 g**

SERVES 4

8 sun-dried tomatoes (not in oil)

1 garlic clove, roughly chopped

large handful of fresh basil leaves, plus a few leaves to garnish

600 ml (1 pint) boiling water

700 g (1 lb 9 oz) red-skinned potatoes, peeled and cut into slices 1 cm (1/2 in) thick

2 red onions, cut into rings

2 tbsp black olives, unpitted

4 x 150 g (5 oz) skinless, boneless cod

1 lemon

salt and freshly ground black pepper

Greek-style Roast Cod

This is a wonderful way to cook – the potatoes are half braised, half roasted, and the steam from the sun-dried tomato stock keeps the fish beautifully moist.

1 Preheat the oven to 220°C/425°F/Gas 7. Place the sun-dried tomatoes, garlic and basil in a mini-chopper or small food processor and whiz until very finely chopped. Stir into the boiling water.

2 Arrange the potato slices and onion rings in a roasting tin and pour over the liquid. Season with salt and pepper and roast for 30 minutes.

3 Once the potatoes are tender, scatter over the olives and arrange the cod fillets on top of the potatoes. Cut four thin slices from the lemon and place one on each fillet. Squeeze over the juice from the rest of the lemon.

4 Season the fish, then return the roasting tin to the oven for 8–10 minutes until the fish is just cooked. Divide between plates and serve.

Nutrition notes per serving
Calories **290** Protein **32.5 g** Carbohydrate **37 g** Fat **2.2 g** Saturated fat **0.4 g** Fibre **3.2 g** Added sugars **none** Salt **0.81 g**

Nutrition notes per serving
Calories **267** Protein **14.9 g** Carbohydrate **12 g** Fat **18.1 g** Saturated fat **4.3 g** Fibre **3.3 g** Added sugars **1.3 g** Salt **2.01 g**

SERVES 4

- 2 tbsp red wine vinegar
- 1 tsp caster sugar
- $^1/_4$ tsp salt
- 1 small red onion, thinly sliced
- 6-cm (2$^1/_2$-inch) piece of cucumber, halved, seeded and thinly sliced into half moons
- pinch of crushed chillies or pink peppercorns
- few torn tarragon leaves
- 230 g packet peppered mackerel
- 100 g packet baby salad leaves
- 400 g can butter beans, drained

Flaked Mackerel and Butter Bean Salad

Mackerel is wonderful. Like salmon, it is an oily fish, and fish oils can play a valuable part in a healthy balanced diet – though of course this does mean these fish aren't low-fat. Bearing this is mind, I've kept the dressing simple and fat-free, so each serving of dressing still only contains 0.1 g of fat.

1 Mix together the vinegar, sugar and salt then stir in the red onion, cucumber, chilli and tarragon and set aside for 10 minutes or so.

2 Meanwhile, skin the fish and break into large flakes. Arrange the fish, baby leaves and butter beans on four serving plates and spoon over the red onion and cucumber dressing.

SERVES 4

500 g (1 lb 2 oz) anya or pink fir-apple potatoes, halved

200 g (7 oz) fine green beans

12 quail's eggs

1 heart of Romaine lettuce, shredded

400 g can tuna in spring water, drained

FOR THE DRESSING

1 tbsp capers, roughly chopped

1 mild red chilli, seeded and finely chopped

1 small garlic clove, crushed

1 tsp olive oil

grated rind and juice of 1 lime

salt and freshly ground black pepper

New Tuna Niçoise

For me, canned tuna always used to be a last resort when the store cupboard had little else to offer, but recently supermarkets have started to stock some lovely new kinds. I particularly like the large flaky tuna fillets in spring water, which have great flavour and texture. Besides cooking, they are also perfect for salads, such as this little classic.

1 Cook the potatoes in a large pan of boiling salted water for 15 minutes, adding the beans to the pan for the last 2–3 minutes of cooking time.

2 Meanwhile, cook the eggs in a pan of boiling water for 4 minutes. Drain well and cool under running water until completely cold.

3 Make the dressing: stir together the capers, chilli, garlic, olive oil and lime rind and juice, adding salt and pepper to taste.

4 Drain the potatoes and beans then cool under running water until completely cold. Shell and halve the eggs.

5 Loosely toss together the lettuce, tuna, potatoes, beans, eggs and dressing. Serve the salad as soon as it is tossed.

Nutrition notes per serving
Calories **198** Protein **16.8 g** Carbohydrate **23 g** Fat **5.1 g** Saturated fat **0.2 g** Fibre **2.8 g** Added sugars **none** Salt **0.36 g**

Poultry and Meat

POULTRY AND MEAT **POULTRY AND MEAT** POULTRY AND MEAT **POULTRY AND**

SERVES 4

- 150 g carton low-fat natural yoghurt
- 2 garlic cloves, crushed
- 1 tsp ground cumin
- 1 tsp chilli powder
- pinch of ground turmeric
- few drops of red food colouring
- 4 bone-in chicken breasts

FOR THE MINT DRIZZLE

- bunch of fresh mint
- 1 small garlic clove, roughly chopped
- 5-cm (2-inch) piece of cucumber, peeled and cubed
- 150 g carton low-fat natural yoghurt
- squeeze of fresh lemon juice
- salt and freshly ground black pepper

Tandoori Chicken with Mint Drizzle

Home-made tandoori chicken is unbelievably easy to prepare and tastes every bit as good as you'd hope for, even if it's cooked in a regular oven rather than a traditional clay tandoor. I don't have a problem with adding a couple of drops of natural red food colouring to get that authentic tandoori look, but by all means leave the colouring out if you prefer. Add your favourite trimmings, such as salad, rice, microwavable poppadoms or chapattis, and finish off your low-fat feast with some zingy mint drizzle.

1 In a large shallow dish, stir together the yoghurt, garlic, cumin, chilli, turmeric, food colouring and some salt and pepper.

2 Remove the skin from the chicken breasts, trim off any visible fat and deeply score each breast. Add the chicken to the marinade and set aside for 30–60 minutes, turning from time to time.

3 To make the drizzle: place the mint, garlic and cucumber in a mini-chopper or food processor and whiz until finely blended. Add the yoghurt and whiz again, then season with lemon juice, salt and pepper. Chill until ready to serve.

4 Preheat the oven to 200°C/400°F/Gas 6. Place the chicken on a non-stick baking sheet and roast for 30 minutes until cooked right through. Serve at once with the mint drizzle.

Nutrition notes per serving
Calories **229** Protein **37.7 g** Carbohydrate **8 g** Fat **5.2 g** Saturated fat **1.9 g** Fibre **0.6 g** Added sugars **none** Salt **0.76 g**

SERVES 4

400 g can chopped tomatoes

300 ml (½ pint) red wine

600 ml (1 pint) chicken stock

8 garlic cloves, finely chopped

4 rosemary sprigs

1 tsp light muscovado sugar

4 x chicken thighs, skinned

4 x chicken drumsticks, skinned

75 g (3 oz) black olives, unpitted

grated rind and juice of 1 orange

200 g (7 oz) piece of French bread, thinly sliced

salt and freshly ground black pepper

Frenchish Chicken and Red Wine Casserole

Low-fat certainly doesn't mean no-fun. This dish, loosely based on a coq au vin, contains quite a quantity of red wine. It takes a while to cook down so save it for the weekend or make it the night before. I top mine with slices of bread but you can serve yours with fat-free mash (page 79) if you prefer.

1 Place the tomatoes, wine, stock, garlic, rosemary and sugar in a flameproof casserole dish and bring to the boil.

2 Meanwhile, pull the skin off the chicken. Add the chicken pieces to the pan. Partially cover and simmer for 1 hour and 20 minutes.

3 Preheat the oven to 200°C/400°F/Gas 6. Add the olives and orange rind and juice to the casserole dish, along with some salt and pepper. Arrange the bread on top of the casserole, then place the dish on a baking sheet.

4 Pop into the oven for 20 minutes until the bread is toasted and golden. The juices will bubble up and dribble down the side and over the bread in places, but don't worry, this is a rustic dish. Serve warm.

Nutrition notes per serving
Calories **409** Protein **39.2 g** Carbohydrate **35 g** Fat **7.9 g** Saturated fat **2.2 g** Fibre **2.7 g** Added sugars **1.3 g** Salt **2.85 g**

Nutrition notes per serving
Calories **461** Protein **41.4 g** Carbohydrate **66 g** Fat **5.3 g** Saturated fat **0.9 g** Fibre **0.7 g** Added sugars **none** Salt **1.47 g**

SERVES 4

4 skinless, boneless chicken breasts, cubed

1 tsp cayenne

1 tsp allspice

1 tsp ground coriander

½ tsp table salt

1 large red onion

2 garlic cloves

1 tbsp sunflower oil

1 tbsp fresh rosemary leaves

300 g (11 oz) basmati rice

750 ml (1¼ pints) hot chicken stock

grated rind and juice of 1 lime

handful of roughly chopped fresh coriander

salt and freshly ground black pepper

mango chutney and poppadoms, to serve

Simple Spiced Chicken Biriyani

A classic one-pot dish. This takes only half an hour to make yet delivers a delicious and satisfying family meal. It's also good for freezing. Serve the biriyani with microwavable poppadoms, which are low in fat. Sprinkle them with a little water and microwave or grill them according to packet instructions. Avoid buying poppadoms that are already cooked as they tend to be fried.

1 Toss together the chicken, spices and salt and set aside for 5 minutes.

2 Meanwhile, slice the onion and garlic. Heat the oil in a large pan, add the chicken, onion and garlic along with some salt and pepper and cook for 5 minutes. Stir in the rosemary leaves and cook for a further 2 minutes until the onions are lightly browned.

3 Add the rice and stock, bring to the boil, then cover and simmer for 12–15 minutes until the rice is tender and the liquid has been absorbed.

4 Stir in the lime rind and juice and the coriander, divide between plates and serve swiftly, with mango chutney and poppadoms on the side.

Angela's Sticky Pork Chops with Fragrant Rice

This dish is a speciality of my friend and fellow food-writer Angela Boggiano. Steaming the pork first tenderizes the meat. This recipe also works very well with chicken fillets, and you'll be pleased to hear that hoisin sauce is low in fat.

1 Place the pork chops in the base of a steamer sat over a pan of boiling water. Cover and steam for 5 minutes.

2 Meanwhile, place the rice in a saucepan with the star anise and cover with water. Bring to the boil and simmer gently for 15 minutes until tender. Drain well.

3 Preheat the grill to high. Stir together the soy, sugar, hoisin and chilli sauces. Place the chops on a rack with a baking sheet underneath and brush the upward-facing side with the mixture. Grill for 3–4 minutes until dark and slightly charred, then turn the chop over, brush the uncooked side with the mixture and grill for a further 3–4 minutes.

4 Serve the sticky chops with the fragrant rice and steamed greens.

Nutrition notes per serving
Calories **337** Protein **22.2 g** Carbohydrate **58 g** Fat **3.4 g** Saturated fat **0.9 g** Fibre **1.3 g** Added sugars **8 g** Salt **2.12 g**

SERVES 4

4 x 75–100 g (3–4 oz) boneless lean loin chops

250 g (9 oz) Thai fragrant rice

1 star anise

2 tbsp soy sauce

1 tbsp dark muscovado sugar

3 tbsp hoisin sauce

1 tbsp chilli sauce

steamed Oriental greens, such as pak choi or choi sum, to serve

SERVES 2

1 tsp sunflower oil

2 chicken breast fillets, cut into strips 1 cm (½ inch) wide

250 g packet mixed baby sweetcorn, carrots and mangetout, halved

4-cm (1½-inch) piece of root ginger, peeled and shredded

4 spring onions, shredded

75 g (3 oz) beansprouts

1 red chilli, seeded, thinly sliced

300 g packet vacuum-packed noodles

1 tsp cornflour

2 tbsp soy sauce

juice of 1 small orange

1 tsp wine vinegar

handful of fresh basil leaves

Chicken and Ginger Stir-fry

Ginger and chicken make for a brilliant stir-fry, and the combination is enhanced further with fresh orange juice.

1 Heat the oil in a wok and when hot add the chicken and stir-fry for 2 minutes. Add the baby vegetables and cook for 3 minutes, then stir in the ginger, spring onions, beansprouts, chilli and noodles and cook for a further 2 minutes.

2 Stir together the cornflour and soy sauce, then mix in the orange juice and vinegar and pour into the pan. Toss all the ingredients together well and cook for a further minute or so until piping hot. Stir in the basil leaves, divide between bowls and serve.

Nutrition notes per serving
Calories **309** Protein **11.2 g** Carbohydrate **58 g** Fat **5.4 g** Saturated fat **0.3 g** Fibre **5.6 g** Added sugars **0.3g** Salt **4.27 g**

Peppered Steaks with Mushroom Yorkshires

A simple variation on a classic Sunday lunch – and it's quick and easy enough to make any day of the week.

1 Preheat the oven to 220°C/425°F/Gas 7. Place a mushroom, stalk-side up, in each hole of a 4-hole non-stick Yorkshire pudding tin. Season with salt and pepper and drizzle a tiny spot of oil over each. Roast for 10 minutes.

2 Meanwhile, place the flour in a bowl, make a well in the centre and beat in the egg, milk and two tablespoons of water to make a smooth batter. Season with salt and pepper.

3 Lift out the mushrooms from the tin, pour in the batter so it comes halfway up each mould, then carefully return each mushroom so it is surrounded by batter. Return to the oven for 20 minutes until risen and dark golden.

4 Preheat a heavy griddle pan or non-stick frying pan. Season the steaks with salt and spread lightly with mustard. Sprinkle over the peppercorns, pressing them well into the steaks. When the Yorkshires are nearly ready, cook the steaks for 3 minutes or so on each side until nicely browned but still a little pink in the centre.

5 Serve each steak and a Yorkshire pudding with mashed potatoes and gravy.

Nutrition notes per serving
Calories **249** Protein **28.4 g** Carbohydrate **18 g** Fat **7.6 g** Saturated fat **2.3 g** Fibre **1.6 g** Added sugars **none** Salt **0.53 g**

SERVES 4

- 4 Portobello field mushrooms
- 1 tsp olive oil
- 75 g (3 oz) plain flour
- 1 egg, beaten
- 5 tbsp skimmed milk
- 4 x 100 g (4 oz) sirloin or rump steaks, fat removed
- 1 tbsp Dijon mustard
- 2 tsp peppercorns, cracked
- salt and freshly ground black pepper
- mashed potatoes and gravy, to serve

HERBED FAT-FREE MASH

Peel and cube white-skinned potatoes, such as Maris Piper, and boil in salted water until tender. Drain well and mash thoroughly, then beat in fat-free fromage frais or skimmed milk and a handful of chopped fresh herbs, such as parsley, basil or chives, until smooth. Season well to taste.

EASY GRAVY

Gravy granules can often be high in fat but old-style powders tend to be low. Alternatively, vigorously bubble a little red wine in a pan for 5 minutes or so then add a stock cube and water. Thicken either with dissolved cornflour or add a spoonful of redcurrant or cranberry jelly, then balance the sweetness with a splash of balsamic vinegar.

Nutrition notes per serving
Calories **130** Protein **17.9 g** Carbohydrate **5 g** Fat **4.3 g** Saturated fat **1.3 g** Fibre **0.1 g** Added sugars **1.3 g** Salt **0.38 g**

SERVES 4

300 g (11 oz) lean rump steak, cut into 16 cubes

1 tsp olive oil

1 tsp ground cumin

1 tsp caster sugar

2 garlic cloves, crushed

3 preserved lemons, quartered, or 6 small lemons, halved

12 pickled chillies (mixed green and red if you can get them)

salt and freshly ground black pepper

warm pitta, salad and reduced-fat hummus, to serve

Spiced Steak Skewers with Preserved Lemon

Preserved lemons are now a common sight in the supermarket and I love the brilliant flavour they can add to the simplest of dishes. Choose lean, tender steak for this, and in summer-time try cooking it over hot coals.

1 In a large bowl, toss together the meat, olive oil, cumin, sugar, garlic and some salt and pepper. Mix well and set aside for 20 minutes.

2 Thread the steak, lemon and chillies onto skewers and grill under a high heat for 5–8 minutes, turning from time to time until well browned but still a little pink in the centre. Serve with warm pitta, salad and hummus.

Lamb and Bulghar Burgers

Pure meat burgers can be very heavy, not to mention high in fat – these are lightened up with bulghar wheat and grated carrot, which give them a touch of Middle Eastern flavour.

1 Place the bulghar wheat in a large bowl and pour over the hot stock. Set aside for 20 minutes until the bulghar is tender, the liquid has been absorbed and the mixture has cooled. Make sure the mixture is not too wet. If the liquid is not fully absorbed, push the mixture through a sieve to drain off any excess.

2 Stir in the minced lamb, onion, carrot, mint and egg, mixing until well blended. Shape into six even-sized burgers then grill or cook in a non-stick frying pan for 3–4 minutes on each side until nicely browned and cooked through, taking care not to break the burgers when turning them. Serve with sauces, salad and buns.

Nutrition notes per serving
Calories **152** Protein **11.8 g** Carbohydrate **15 g** Fat **4.9 g** Saturated fat **2.0 g** Fibre **0.7 g**
Added sugars **none** Salt **0.24 g**

SERVES 6

- 100 g (4 oz) bulghar wheat
- 200 ml (7 fl oz) hot chicken stock
- 250 g (9 oz) lean minced lamb
- 1 small onion, finely chopped
- 1 large carrot, finely grated
- large handful of fresh mint, finely chopped
- 1 egg, beaten
- crusty bread buns, salad and tomato ketchup or sweet chilli sauce, to serve

SERVES 4

- 700 g jar passata
- 2 tsp dark muscovado sugar
- grated rind and juice of 1 lemon (keep them separate)
- 2 garlic cloves, roughly chopped
- 1 red chilli, seeded and roughly chopped
- small bunch of parsley, roughly chopped
- 75 g (3 oz) crustless white bread
- 250 g (9 oz) lean minced pork
- 1 egg
- 300 g (11 oz) pasta shapes, such as spirals or penne
- 2 tbsp freshly grated Parmesan
- salt and freshly ground black pepper

Crusty Meatball Pasta

I always think meatballs should be coated in a smooth sauce, which is why I've opted for passata, which is just sieved tomatoes. If you've got canned plum tomatoes in the cupboard just liquidise two 400g cans and use them instead. And although I've used pork, any lean mince would be fine.

1 Place the passata, sugar and lemon juice in a pan and heat gently.

2 Meanwhile, place the garlic, chilli, parsley and lemon rind in a food processor and whiz until finely chopped. Add the bread and whiz to make crumbs. Finally add the mince, egg and some salt and pepper and pulse briefly until well blended – take care not to overblend or the mixture will lose its texture.

3 Shape the mixture into 20 small balls and drop them into the sauce. Simmer gently for 20 minutes.

4 Meanwhile, preheat the oven to 220°C/425°F/Gas 7. Cook the pasta in a pan of boiling salted water according to packet instructions.

5 Drain the pasta, toss with the meatball sauce then turn into a heatproof dish. Scatter over the Parmesan and a good grinding of black pepper and bake for 20 minutes until the top is crusty and golden.

Nutrition notes per serving
Calories **431** Protein **20.2 g** Carbohydrate **80 g** Fat **5.6 g** Saturated fat **1.8 g** Fibre **3.1 g** Added sugars **5.2 g** Salt **1.34 g**

SERVES 4

4 thick slices of granary bread, cubed
4 rashers lean back bacon, chopped
juice of 1/2 lemon
1 large ripe avocado
100 g (4 oz) rosebud beetroots in vinegar, drained
125 g carton bocconcini (baby mozzarella)
100 g packet baby spinach and watercress salad
salt and freshly ground black pepper

Avocado and Baby Beetroot Salad with Crispy Bacon

Yes, I know avocado is high in natural oils, but it is also rich in vitamin E and the B-complex vitamins, which are brilliant for you. It tastes lovely, too, and don't forget, we're only using one for four servings. Rosebud beetroot are the smallest size of beetroot and are available in jars from the supermarket. I like to serve this salad just slightly warm, but you may prefer to let everything cool before you assemble it.

1 Preheat the oven to 200°C/400°F/Gas 6. Scatter the bread cubes over a non-stick baking sheet, ensuring they fall in a single layer. Bake for 15–20 minutes until crisp and golden brown.

2 Meanwhile, cook the bacon in a non-stick frying pan until crispy, then remove from the heat. Squeeze the lemon juice over the bacon.

3 Peel, halve, stone and dice the avocado and add to the bacon along with the beetroots and bocconcini.

4 Divide the leaves between four serving bowls and spoon over the avocado mixture. Scatter over the crunchy croûtons and serve.

Nutrition notes per serving
Calories **311** Protein **17.5 g** Carbohydrate **21 g** Fat **17.9 g** Saturated fat **6.0 g** Fibre **4.1 g** Added sugars **none** Salt **2.17 g**

SUPER HEALTHY

Cauliflower and Chilli Pasta

A regular supper dish in my household, this is satisfying as well as packed with vitamins and fibre. For extra crunch and a bit of sizzle, I top mine with toasted breadcrumbs.

1 Cut the cauliflower into small florets, adding the smaller tender green leaves too. Cook in a large pan of boiling salted water for 5 minutes then add the pasta and continue to cook for 12–15 minutes according to packet instructions.

2 Meanwhile, heat the oil in a small non-stick frying pan and cook the onion, garlic and chilli for 3–4 minutes until softened. Add the tomatoes and cook for a couple of minutes until softened and pulpy. Add a ladle of the cooking water, stirring to moisten the tomato mixture, then season with salt and pepper.

3 Drain the pasta and cauliflower quite loosely so the cauliflower retains some of the moisture. Return to the pan and stir in the tomato sauce. Divide between bowls and serve straight away.

Nutrition notes per serving
Calories **516** Protein **19.8 g** Carbohydrate **102 g** Fat **6.2 g** Saturated fat **0.8 g** Fibre **6.7 g**
Added sugars **none** Salt **0.07 g**

SERVES 4

- 1 small cauliflower
- 500 g packet chunky pasta shapes, such as penne or conchiglie
- 1 tbsp olive oil
- 1 small onion, finely chopped
- 2 garlic cloves, finely chopped
- 2 red chillies, finely chopped
- 2 tomatoes, roughly chopped
- salt and freshly ground black pepper

FOR THE CRISPY CRUMBS

Heat a non-stick frying pan and cook a handful of fresh white breadcrumbs over a medium heat, shaking the pan until the crumbs are crisp and golden.

SERVES 6

1 tbsp olive oil
1 large red onion, finely chopped
2 garlic cloves, finely chopped
4 fresh thyme sprigs
500 g (1 lb 2 oz) risotto rice
200 ml (7 fl oz) dry white wine
1 litre ($1^{3}/_{4}$ pints) hot vegetable stock
2 x 410 g cans of cannellini beans, drained and rinsed
2 tbsp freshly grated Parmesan
freshly ground black pepper

Cannellini Bean and Red Onion Risotto

It's hard to think of any food more comforting than a soft and creamy-textured risotto. Cannellini beans also have a wonderful creamy texture, which lends itself well to this dish. Use your favourite risotto rice – mine is carnaroli.

1 Heat the oil in a large pan and gently cook the onion, garlic and thyme for 5 minutes until softened. Add the rice, stir for a few seconds then pour in the wine.

2 Bubble rapidly until the wine evaporates, then slowly add the stock in batches, letting the rice absorb the liquid each time before adding more. Add the beans about halfway through – keep the heat fairly high and the whole process should take about 20 minutes.

3 Season with pepper. Once all the liquid has been absorbed and the grains are soft and creamy, divide the risotto between bowls. Top each serving with a sprinkling of Parmesan and a good grinding of black pepper and serve swiftly.

Nutrition notes per serving
Calories **435** Protein **15.5 g** Carbohydrate **83 g** Fat **4.4 g** Saturated fat **1 g** Fibre **6.4 g** Added sugars **none** Salt **1.53 g**

SERVES 2

200 g (7 oz) new potatoes, sliced

5 eggs

1 garlic clove, thinly sliced

4 spring onions, thinly sliced

1 tsp chopped fresh rosemary or pinch of dried

1 tsp olive oil

100 g (4 oz) frozen broad beans, thawed and shelled

50 g (2 oz) feta

sea salt and freshly ground black pepper

tomato salad, to serve

Broad Bean and Feta Tortilla

This is an excellent high-protein supper dish with carbohydrates from the potatoes for extra energy and broad beans for iron, fibre and vitamin C. Serve with a tomato salad for a perfectly balanced and very tasty meal.

1 Cook the potatoes in a large pan of boiling salted water for 5 minutes until just tender.

2 Crack the eggs into a large bowl and beat well together with a splash of water. Stir the garlic, spring onions and rosemary into the eggs with a little salt and plenty of black pepper.

3 Heat the oil in a 20-cm (8-inch) non-stick skillet or frying pan. Drain the potatoes well and stir into the egg mixture along with the broad beans. Pour into the hot pan and cook for 1 minute or so, stirring until the egg begins to set.

4 Crumble the feta into small pieces and scatter over the top of the tortilla. Cook for 6–7 minutes until the egg is almost completely set. Preheat the grill to medium.

5 Place the pan under the preheated grill for 2–3 minutes until the tortilla is golden brown on top. Slide it onto a chopping board and cut into wedges. Transfer the tortilla wedges to plates and serve with the tomato salad.

Nutrition notes per serving
Calories **405** Protein **27.8 g** Carbohydrate **21 g** Fat **23.7 g** Saturated fat **7.9 g** Fibre **4.4 g** Added sugars **none** Salt **1.48 g**

SERVES 4

500 g packet chunky pasta shapes, such as penne or conchiglie

400 g can artichoke hearts in brine, drained

1 garlic clove, roughly chopped

1 tbsp toasted pine nuts

juice of 1/2 lemon

2 tbsp snipped chives

salt and freshly ground black pepper

Pasta with Artichoke Sauce

Canned artichokes are fantastic – they have a great flavour and texture and purée really well for dips and sauces. Make sure you choose the ones canned in brine and not the ones in olive oil in jars.

1 Cook the pasta in a large pan of salted boiling water according to packet instructions.

2 Meanwhile, place the artichokes, garlic and pine nuts in a mini-chopper or small food processor and whiz to form a coarse purée. Add lemon juice and salt and pepper to taste then stir in the snipped chives.

3 Drain the pasta well, toss with the sauce, divide between bowls and serve.

Nutrition notes per serving
Calories **470** Protein **16.5 g** Carbohydrate **97 g** Fat **4.4 g** Saturated fat **0.6 g** Fibre **5 g** Added sugars **none** Salt **0.25 g**

Nutrition notes per serving
Calories **312** Protein **17 g** Carbohydrate **49 g** Fat **6.8 g** Saturated fat **2.8 g** Fibre **5.4 g** Added sugars **1.8 g** Salt **2.09 g**

SERVES 4

290 g packet pizza dough mix

1 quantity simple tomato sauce, cooled (see recipe on page 101), or 200 g (7 oz) passata

3 ripe figs, quartered

150 g (5 oz) ball reduced-fat mozzarella, cubed

4 jalapeño chillies, sliced, seeds and all

freshly ground black pepper

Fig and Jalapeño Pizza

I love making pizza dough from scratch, but packet mixes do save quite a bit of time and give good results, so they are ideal for midweek meals. Jalapeño chillies are the short, fat green ones you so often see around. They have a gentle kick rather than a fiery heat, and the contrast with the sweetness of the figs is fantastic.

1 Preheat the oven to 200°C/400°F/Gas 6. Empty the pizza dough mix into a bowl and make up with warm water according to packet instructions. Knead vigorously on a floured surface for 5 minutes until smooth.

2 Roll out the dough to make a 12-cm (5-inch) circle – this may end up more like an oval, depending on how big a baking sheet you've got. Lightly dust your largest baking sheet with flour, then transfer the pizza base to it.

3 Spread the sauce over the dough, then scatter the figs, mozzarella and jalapeños on top. Grind over some black pepper then set aside for 10–15 minutes to rise.

4 Bake for 20–25 minutes until risen and golden brown. Cut into wedges and serve.

Everyday Tagine

A tagine is a spicy North African stew, with a touch of sweetness that often comes from fruit. This one is easy to make and is quite brothy – perfect for couscous, which soaks up all the lovely juices.

1 Place the couscous in a large bowl and just cover with boiling water. Stir well then set aside for 10 minutes.

2 Meanwhile, heat the oil in a large sauté pan and stir-fry the onions, sweet potato and aubergine for 5–10 minutes, stirring frequently until well browned. Add the tomatoes and cumin seeds and cook for 2 minutes.

3 Add the stock to the pan with the apricots, chickpeas, chilli and cinnamon stick. Simmer gently for 15 minutes until the vegetables are tender.

4 Cut four thin slices of lime. Squeeze the juice from the rest of the lime into the tagine and stir in the mint. Season to taste.

5 Divide the couscous between serving bowls, spoon over the tagine and garnish with the lime slices.

Nutrition notes per serving
Calories **377** Protein **12.9 g** Carbohydrate **71 g** Fat **6.3 g** Saturated fat **0.7 g** Fibre **8.5 g** Added sugars **none** Salt **1.26 g**

SERVES 4

- 250 g (9 oz) couscous
- 1 tbsp olive oil
- 2 onions, thickly sliced
- 1 sweet or ordinary potato, peeled and cubed
- 1 large aubergine, cubed
- 2 tomatoes, roughly chopped
- 1/2 tsp cumin seeds
- 1 litre (1 3/4 pints) hot vegetable stock
- 100 g (4 oz) small dried apricots
- 400 g can chickpeas, drained
- 1/2 tsp dried chilli flakes
- 1 cinnamon stick
- 1 lime
- handful of fresh mint leaves, roughly chopped
- salt and freshly ground black pepper

Nutrition notes per serving
Calories **285** Protein **8.9 g** Carbohydrate **64 g** Fat **1.1 g** Saturated fat **0.1 g** Fibre **4.3 g** Added sugars **none** Salt **0.23 g**

SERVES 4

400 g can chopped tomatoes

1 shallot, finely chopped

2 garlic cloves, finely chopped

1 sprig of fresh rosemary or thyme, or a couple of bay leaves

pinch of crushed chillies (optional)

60 g packet wild rocket

FOR THE GNOCCHI

500 g (1 lb 2 oz) waxy potatoes such as red skins or new potatoes, peeled and diced

15 g (½ oz) fresh basil leaves, finely chopped

200 g (7 oz) plain flour

salt and freshly ground black pepper

Basil Gnocchi with Simple Tomato Sauce and Wild Rocket

Home-made gnocchi are truly delicious and much easier to prepare than you might imagine. Shop-bought, vacuum-packed ones are fine to serve with a simple sauce like this if you're short of time, but they won't match up in terms or flavour or texture.

1 Begin with the sauce: place the tomatoes in a small pan, then half fill the can with water and add that to the pan. Stir in the shallot, garlic, herbs, chillies and salt and pepper. Bring to the boil and simmer gently for at least an hour until thickened and dark red.

2 Meanwhile, to make the gnocchi, boil the potatoes for 10–15 minutes until tender, then drain. Mash them well – this bit is important because lumps will be noticeable in the gnocchi, so use a potato ricer if you have one, or mash the potatoes thoroughly to as smooth a texture as possible.

3 Sprinkle over the basil, plenty of salt and pepper and the flour. Using a wooden spoon or your hands, bring together to make a firm dough. Knead the dough gently for a couple of minutes then roll out into sausages about 1 cm (½ inch) thick. Cut the sausages into pieces 2.5 cm (1 inch) long.

4 Gently cook the gnocchi in a pan of simmering water for a minute or two until they rise to the surface. Scoop them out as they rise, toss with the tomato sauce and rocket leaves, and serve.

Curried Vegetable Hotpot with Turmeric Dumplings

Few dishes are more comforting than stew and dumplings. This is a flavour-packed spiced stew, and the dumplings are made with a little sunflower oil in place of the traditional vegetable suet.

1 Place the stock, ginger and cumin seeds in a large pan. Add the vegetables, including the tomatoes, the curry paste and some salt and pepper, bring to the boil and simmer for 20 minutes.

2 Meanwhile, make the dumplings. In a large bowl, mix together the flour, baking powder, turmeric, table salt and coriander. Make a well in the centre and add the oil and milk, then bring together to make a soft dough.

3 Roll the dough into sixteen balls and drop them gently into the pan. Cover and cook without stirring for 7–8 minutes until the dumplings are puffed and cooked through and the vegetables are tender.

4 Stir in the lemon juice and check the seasoning. Ladle into bowls and serve.

Nutrition notes per serving
Calories **470** Protein **17 g** Carbohydrate **87 g** Fat **8.2 g** Saturated fat **0.9 g** Fibre **11.9 g** Added sugars **none** Salt **2.31 g**

SERVES 4

- 1.2 litres (2 pints) vegetable stock
- 1 tsp freshly grated root ginger
- 2 tsp toasted cumin seeds
- 1.5 kg (3 lb) sturdy vegetables, cut into large chunks, e.g. potatoes, carrots, pumpkin, cauliflower, parsnips, leeks
- 1 tomato, roughly chopped
- 1 tbsp hot curry paste
- juice of 1/2 lemon
- salt and freshly ground black pepper

FOR THE DUMPLINGS

- 250 g (9 oz) plain flour
- 1 tsp baking powder
- 1/2 tsp ground turmeric
- 1/2 tsp table salt
- 2 tbsp finely chopped fresh coriander
- 1 tbsp sunflower oil
- 150 ml (5 fl oz) semi-skimmed milk

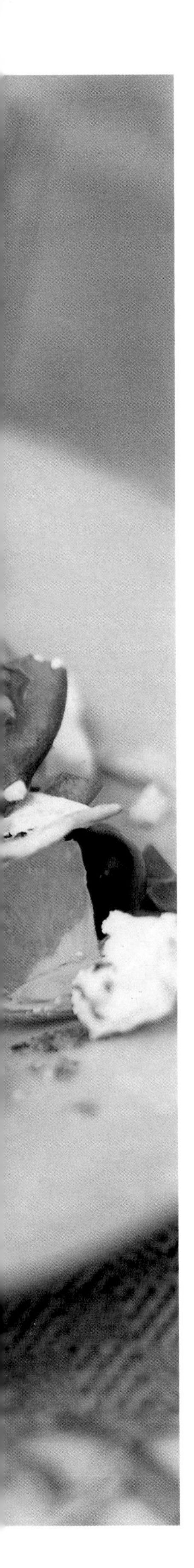

SERVES 4

1 tsp coriander seeds
1 tbsp olive oil
juice and grated rind of 1 lime
4 ripe tomatoes, quartered
4 spring onions, finely chopped
1 garlic clove, finely chopped
2 oranges, peeled and cut into pieces
75 g (3 oz) small black olives
2 flour tortillas
100 g (4 oz) feta, crumbled
handful of fresh coriander leaves
salt and freshly ground black pepper

Middle-Eastern Salad with Orange and Feta

This is a wonderful, stylish salad, based on a classic Middle-Eastern dish called a *fattoush*. Make it in the summer when tomatoes are sweet.

1 In a large non-stick frying pan, toast the coriander seeds until they turn golden and release their aroma. Empty them into a cup and smash roughly with the end of a rolling pin. Stir in the olive oil, lime rind and juice and some salt and pepper.

2 Place the tomatoes, spring onions, garlic, oranges and olives in a large serving dish and pour over the dressing. Stir well and set aside.

3 Toast the flour tortillas, one at a time, in the frying pan used for the coriander, then tear the bread into small pieces. Stir into the salad, along with the feta and coriander leaves, and serve.

Nutrition notes per serving
Calories **232** Protein **8.1 g** Carbohydrate **28 g** Fat **10.8 g** Saturated fat **3.9 g** Fibre **3.6 g**
Added sugars **none** Salt **2.22 g**

Rice Noodle Salad with Lemon Tofu

I'm a big fan of tofu – it's naturally low in fat, has a lovely texture and takes on flavours really well. If you have time, leave the tofu in its marinade for a good couple of hours, then assemble the salad just before you want to serve it. To toast the sesame seeds, place them in a non-stick frying pan over a medium heat and cook them, stirring, for a couple of minutes until lightly browned.

1 In a large bowl, mix together the soy sauce, lemon rind and juice, chillies and two tablespoons of water. Add the tofu cubes and leave to marinate for at least 30 minutes.

2 Place the noodles in a large bowl, cover with boiling water and set aside for 5 minutes or so. Drain and cool under running water.

3 Toss together the cooled noodles, mangetout, radishes, red onion and sesame seeds. Gently stir in the tofu and marinade and divide between bowls. Scatter over the coriander leaves and serve.

Nutrition notes per serving
Calories **247** Protein **10.2 g** Carbohydrate **45 g** Fat **4.1 g** Saturated fat **0.6 g** Fibre **1.1 g**
Added sugars **0.2 g** Salt **2.07 g**

SERVES 4

- 3 tbsp light soy sauce
- grated rind and juice of 1 lemon
- 2 bird's-eye red chillies, thinly sliced
- 300 g packet firm tofu, cubed
- 200 g (7 oz) fine rice noodles
- 100 g (4 oz) mangetout, halved lengthways
- bunch of radishes, thinly sliced
- 1 small red onion, thinly sliced
- 1 tsp toasted sesame seeds
- handful of fresh coriander leaves

Roasted Banana Cheesecake

Ricotta is low in fat and I like its texture, but you could use cottage cheese in this cake instead, only pass it through a sieve first. The classic dense cheesecake texture and scrumptious combination of bananas, ginger and sultanas are wonderful.

1 Preheat the oven to 200°C/400°F/Gas 6. Place the bananas on a baking sheet and roast for 15 minutes or until the skins blacken and the bananas feel soft – this time may vary depending on how ripe your bananas are. Peel the bananas, mash with a fork and leave to cool.

2 Reduce the oven temperature to 180°C/350°F/Gas 4. In a large bowl combine the ricotta, sugar, cornflour and eggs and beat with an electric whisk until smooth. Stir in the mashed banana, ginger and sultanas.

3 Pour the mixture into a 23-cm (9-inch) non-stick springform cake tin, place on a baking sheet and bake for 40–45 minutes until golden – it will still feel a little wobbly but will set as it cools.

4 Turn off the oven, open the door and leave the cheesecake in the oven until completely cool. Then chill for at least an hour or two in the tin, before cutting into wedges to serve.

Nutrition notes per serving
Calories **255** Protein **10 g** Carbohydrate **32 g** Fat **10.4 g** Saturated fat **5.8 g** Fibre **0.6 g** Added sugars **13.4 g** Salt **0.27 g**

SERVES 10

- **4 bananas**
- **750 g (1 lb 11 oz) ricotta cheese**
- **125 g (4½ oz) caster sugar**
- **2 tbsp cornflour**
- **3 large eggs**
- **2 pieces of stem ginger in syrup, drained and finely chopped**
- **75 g (3 oz) sultanas**

Nutrition notes per serving
Calories **189** Protein **6.1 g** Carbohydrate **32 g** Fat **4.9 g** Saturated fat **1.4 g** Fibre **0.1 g** Added sugars **26.3 g** Salt **0.17 g**

SERVES 8

- **200 g (7 oz) caster sugar**
- **600 ml (1 pint) fresh orange juice**
- **6 eggs, beaten**

Spanish Orange Crème Caramels

I love these little puddings – they're like crème caramels only made with freshly squeezed orange juice instead of cream. The orange and the dark caramel make a fantastic combination. They benefit from a night in the fridge so that the hard caramel base can slowly melt into a syrup – which means they are perfect for dinner parties because you can make them in advance. I make mine in terracotta dishes and give one to each guest along with a small plate for turning the pudding out on. Sometimes a disc of caramel stays stuck in the base of the dish and you'll find that some guests like to scrape it with a teaspoon long after dinner has ended, unwilling to let any go to waste.

1 Preheat the oven to 180°C/350°F/Gas 4. Place half the sugar in a small pan with 100 ml (4 fl oz) water and cook gently, stirring from time to time, until the sugar dissolves. Once the sugar has completely dissolved, raise the heat and bubble rapidly until the mixture starts to caramelize. Be brave – the darker the syrup gets, the more wonderful the flavour, but don't let it burn.

2 Carefully pour the caramel into eight moulds, swirling it round the sides so it goes up the edges, then place in a roasting tin.

3 Beat together the orange juice, eggs and remaining sugar, then carefully pour into the moulds. Pour boiling water into the tin so it comes three-quarters of the way up the sides of the moulds. Bake for 20 minutes until just set, then allow to cool.

4 Cover and chill for several hours or overnight until ready to turn out and serve.

SERVES 6

200 g carton half-fat crème fraîche

200 g carton fat-free Greek-style natural yoghurt

2 tbsp orange-flower water or rose water

540 g can rhubarb in syrup

1–2 tbsp icing sugar (optional)

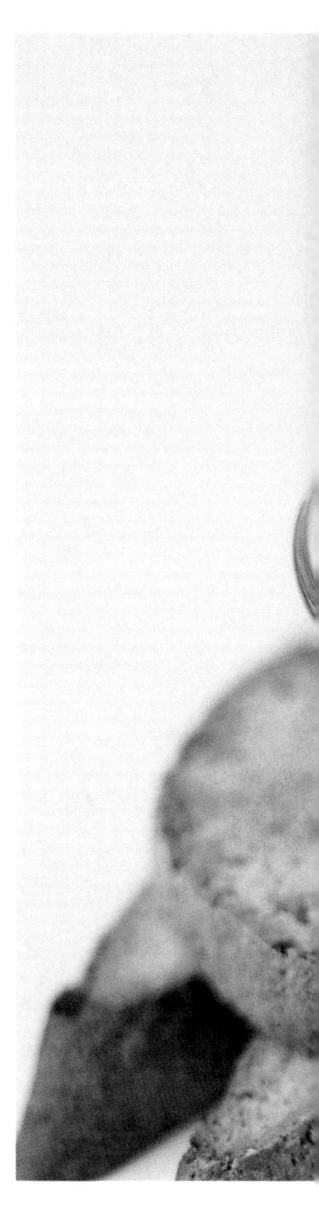

Rhubarb and Orange-flower Fool

I have no problem with canned fruit – it has saved me on many occasions. But if rhubarb is in season, then do stew down the fresh stuff with a little sugar. This is good for making ahead and chilling until you are ready to serve it. I like to serve a couple of biscuits on the side for added texture – Italian cantuccini biscuits are made without added fat. They are easy to get hold of, but also easy – and nicer – to make yourself (see below).

1 Stir together the crème fraîche, yoghurt and flower water.

2 Drain the rhubarb and stir the fruit into the fool mixture. If you wish, add a tablespoon or two of icing sugar to taste.

3 Spoon into small glasses, then cover and chill until ready to serve.

Nutrition notes per serving
Calories **131** Protein **3.8 g** Carbohydrate **12 g** Fat **8 g** Saturated fat **5 g** Fibre **0.7 g** Added sugars **8.8 g** Salt **0.16 g**

ROSEMARY CANTUCCINI

Combine 225 g (8 oz) plain flour, 175 g (6 oz) golden caster sugar, a pinch of salt and ½ teaspoon of baking powder in a large bowl. Make a well in the centre and stir in 2 beaten eggs, a few drops of pure vanilla extract, the grated rind of 1 lemon and 2 teaspoons of chopped fresh rosemary leaves.

Shape loosely into two logs and transfer to a non-stick baking sheet (spaced well apart). Bake at 200°C/400°F/Gas 6 for 20–25 minutes until pale golden and set.

Using a serrated knife, cut the logs on the diagonal into slices 1 cm (½ inch) thick. Arrange on the baking sheet and return to the oven for 5 minutes until golden. Transfer to a wire rack and leave to cool and harden.

Nutrition notes per serving
Calories **113** Protein **4.5 g** Carbohydrate **22 g** Fat **1.3 g** Saturated fat **0.8 g** Fibre **0.3 g** Added sugars **14.4 g** Salt **0.24 g**

SERVES 6

- 400 ml carton reduced-fat fresh custard
- 3 tbsp icing sugar
- grated rind of 2 limes
- pulp and seeds from 3 ripe passion fruit
- 3 egg whites
- 1 tbsp caster sugar

Lime and Passion Fruit Soufflé

This is a cheat's version of a soufflé but it works really well. My friend the chef Paul Merrett taught me to glaze the soufflé before baking it – this works because it gives the soufflé a flat surface to push up against and helps get a good rise as well as a pretty finish. Remember, it will start to deflate moments after it comes out of the oven, so have your guests ready and waiting at the table.

1 Preheat the oven to 190°C/375°F/Gas 5 and the grill to medium. Place the custard in a large bowl and stir in the icing sugar, lime rind and passion fruit.

2 In a separate bowl, whisk the egg whites until stiff. Using a large metal spoon, gently fold the egg whites into the custard. Carefully transfer the mixture to a large soufflé dish, level off the surface and sprinkle with the caster sugar.

3 Pop the soufflé under a medium grill for 3 minutes until the sugar melts. Transfer to the oven and bake for 20 minutes until well risen and set. Serve swiftly.

SERVES 6

4 egg whites
pinch of salt
225 g (8 oz) golden caster sugar
1 tsp cornflour
1/2 tsp pure vanilla extract
1 tsp white wine vinegar
25 g (1 oz) cocoa powder
425 g can pitted black cherries in syrup
200 g carton fat-free fromage frais

Chocolate Meringues with Cherry Ripple

The combination of chocolate and cherries is delicious, and I like to use the Pavlova method of making meringues – the addition of cornflour and vinegar gives you that lovely mallowy centre. Cherries are in season for such a short time that I've used canned ones for this so you can make it at any time of year.

1 Preheat the oven to 140°C/275°F/Gas 1. Whisk the egg whites with the pinch of salt until very stiff. Gradually add the sugar to make a stiff shiny mixture. Stir together the cornflour, vanilla and vinegar and whisk in. Sift over the cocoa then whisk in.

2 Spoon twelve oval shapes onto two baking sheets lined with silicone or Teflon paper. Bake for 45 minutes until the outer shell is crisp but the centre still feels a little soft. Carefully peel off the paper and leave to cool.

3 Meanwhile, drain the cherries, pouring the syrup into a small saucepan. Bring the syrup to the boil and bubble rapidly for 7–8 minutes until thick. Set aside to cool.

4 Stir the cherries into the fromage frais. Spoon the mixture onto six of the meringues, then drizzle over the thickened syrup. Cover with the remaining meringue halves, and serve soon.

Nutrition notes per serving
Calories **243** Protein **6 g** Carbohydrate **56 g** Fat **1 g** Saturated fat **0.6 g** Fibre **0.9 g** Added sugars **45.5 g** Salt **0.44 g**

SERVES 6

1.2 litres (2 pints) semi-skimmed milk

75 g (3 oz) golden caster sugar, plus extra for dusting

8 cardamom pods, cracked

1 vanilla pod

150 g (5 oz) Thai jasmine rice

Vanilla and Cardamom Rice Pudding

It's hard to beat a proper home-baked rice pudding. I make mine with semi-skimmed milk for the creamy texture, but you can make it with skimmed if you wish. I love to use fragrant Thai jasmine rice but, again, use traditional pudding rice if you prefer it. The dish is very easy – just put it in the oven before you sit down to dinner. Spoon any leftovers into a small bowl and serve chilled the next day.

1 Preheat the oven to 160°C/325°F/Gas 3. Put the milk, sugar and cardamom pods in a pan. Split the vanilla pod and scrape out the seeds. Add the pod and seeds to the pan and stir over a gentle heat until the sugar has dissolved, then bring to a simmer.

2 Scatter the rice over the bottom of a 1.75-litre (3-pint) ovenproof dish. Pour the milky mixture over the rice. Stir well, cover with foil then bake for 1 hour, until almost all the liquid has been absorbed and the rice is tender.

3 Preheat the grill to hot. A skin will have formed on the surface of the rice pudding – carefully lift this off and discard it. Dust the pudding with a little more caster sugar and place under the hot grill until brown and bubbling. Serve warm, or chilled the next day.

Nutrition notes per serving
Calories **229** Protein **8.6 g** Carbohydrate **44 g** Fat **3.4 g** Saturated fat **2 g** Fibre **0.4 g** Added sugars **14 g** Salt **0.29 g**

SERVES 6

- 1 small egg white
- 50 g (2 oz) caster sugar
- 3 tbsp maple syrup
- 1 tsp ground ginger
- 75 g (3 oz) plain flour
- 750 g (1 lb 11 oz) strawberries, halved if large, and vanilla sugar (optional), to serve

Maple Wafers with Strawberries

Strawberries are great for you, not only are they juicy and delicious, they're also a good source of folate and potassium, and a very good source of fibre and Vitamin C.

1 Preheat the oven to 180°C/350°F/Gas 4. In a large bowl, lightly whisk the egg white until frothy, then stir in the sugar, syrup, ginger and flour to make a thick paste.

2 Line one large or two small baking sheets with silicone paper. Using the back of a spoon, spread the mixture thinly over the paper into eighteen circles, each with a diameter of about 8 cm (3 inches).

3 Bake for 5 minutes until pale golden. Allow to cool for a few moments. Then, using a palette knife, lift off the wafers, transfer to a wire rack and leave them to cool and harden.

4 Place the strawberries in a bowl and sprinkle over a little sugar if desired. Set aside at room temperature until ready to serve with the maple wafers.

Nutrition notes per serving
Calories **149** Protein **3.1 g** Carbohydrate **32 g** Fat **2 g** Saturated fat **0.5 g** Fibre **1.8 g** Added sugars **8.8 g** Salt **0.03 g**

Nutrition notes per serving
Calories **146** Protein **5.6 g** Carbohydrate **19 g** Fat **6 g** Saturated fat **0.8 g** Fibre **1.7 g** Added sugars **12.2 g** Salt **0.14 g**

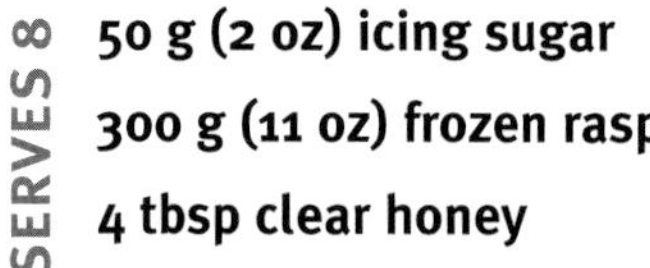

SERVES 8

50 g (2 oz) icing sugar

300 g (11 oz) frozen raspberries

4 tbsp clear honey

500 g (1 lb 2 oz) low-fat natural yoghurt

75 g (3 oz) unblanched almonds

Honey, Almond and Raspberry Yoghurt Ice

This is a delicious dessert, frozen in a loaf tin. After the dish has frozen, remove the tin and cut off slices whenever you want to serve it, just remember to wrap up the remainder with freezer film before you return it to the freezer. All nuts contain oils, but remember, these are the right kind of oils and shouldn't be excluded from your diet completely. Nuts contain useful fibre too.

1 Line a standard 900 g (2 lb) loaf tin with freezer film. Sift the icing sugar over the frozen raspberries in a bowl, then drizzle over the honey. Stir well together, then mix in the yoghurt and almonds.

2 Spoon into the lined loaf tin, levelling off the surface. Cover the top with freezer film and freeze overnight.

3 Turn out of the tin and, using a serrated or electric knife, cut into slices.

SERVES 8

225 g (8 oz) caster sugar
50 g (2 oz) cocoa powder
2 tbsp instant coffee granules
1/2 tsp ground cinnamon
600 ml (1 pint) water

Mocha Granita

I've always been a fan of the granita – easier to make than a sorbet, and a fraction of the calories of ice cream. If you make this a few days ahead, there is a chance it will harden in the freezer and be difficult to serve. If this happens, just whiz it in the food processor to break up the crystals again.

1 Place the sugar, cocoa, coffee and cinnamon in a pan and stir to combine.

2 Add a little of the water, stirring to make a paste. (Don't add all the water at once or you will never get the lumps out.) Add the rest of the water, then put the pan over the heat and bring to the boil, stirring until the sugar dissolves. Leave to cool.

3 Strain the liquid into a rigid container and freeze for 2 hours until almost firm. Using a fork, break the mixture into large flaky crystals. Freeze for a further 2 hours, then break it up again. Spoon into small tumblers and serve.

Nutrition notes per serving
Calories **130** Protein **1.4 g** Carbohydrate **30 g** Fat **1.4 g** Saturated fat **0.8 g** Fibre **0.8 g** Added sugars **28.9 g** Salt **0.16 g**

SERVES 4

- 3 large peaches, halved, stoned and sliced
- 2 tbsp Amaretto or other nut liqueur
- 2 tbsp golden caster sugar
- 4–6 large sheets of filo pastry
- 125 g (4½ oz) raspberries

Peach Melba Tarts

Peaches and raspberries are a well-known wonderful match. Here they're spooned into crisp little filo pastry cases and served warm. Filo is low in fat so use it in place of short-crust or puff pastry when it comes to making tarts and pies

1 Preheat the oven to 200°C/400°F/Gas 6. Arrange the peaches on a baking sheet and drizzle over the liqueur, then two tablespoons of water. Sprinkle with the sugar, and roast for 15 minutes.

2 Meanwhile, cut each sheet of filo into even-sized 10-cm (4-inch) squares – you will need 18 altogether. Use the filo squares to line six tart tins, three squares per tin, laying them at angles, one on top of the next with the corners sticking up. Place a ball of crumpled foil in each tart case and bake for 4–5 minutes until golden.

3 Add the raspberries to the peaches and return to the oven for a further 5 minutes.

4 Remove the foil and place a tart case on each of six small serving plates. Spoon the peaches, raspberries and any cooking juices into the cases and serve straight away.

Nutrition notes per serving
Calories **148** Protein **3.2 g** Carbohydrate **32 g** Fat **1.1 g** Saturated fat **0.2 g** Fibre **1.8 g** Added sugars **7.6 g** Salt **0.46 g**

Index

Page numbers in *italic* refer to the illustrations